faith and gasoline
a devotional journey
a story about the road we share together.

faith and gasoline
a devotional journey
a story about the road we share together.

by davepettigrew

somebody else's press
New York, New York

TABLE OF CONTENTS

For Rosie, Marco & Sam.
Thank you.

faith and gasoline
a devotional journey

Chapter 1
LOVE IS HERE

CHAPTER 1:
Love Is Here

It's cold this morning. I can feel the frost on the handle of the car as I pull it to open the door. I sit behind the wheel and my breath clouds my vision as I exhale. This journey, this trip, will be unlike any other. The road ahead is long, I know that, but I'm ready to take it. I turn the engine over and shift the car into drive. I hear the crackle of the sand under the tires as I pull onto the highway.

I head towards a nearby diner. Coffee. Breakfast. The little things make the big things easier. The waitress who serves me is helpful. A warm, welcoming smile greets me as I sit down. She walks over and takes my order. I hear the clank of silverware, the low rumble of conversation in other booths. Other lives working through the problems of life, the joys of life. My mind wanders as I gaze out the window. I finish my meal and I turn towards the waitress as she brings the check, "Long day ahead of you?" she asks. I say yeah and she cracks that smile again. "Don't worry, each one of us is on our own journey, just be thankful that we're not alone." I ask what she means. "We're all in this together, there's nothing that will happen to you today that hasn't happened to someone before." Diner waitress wisdom. I smile and nod my head. She continues, "There's a love that holds it all together, we all have access to it, just some of us don't want to let it in." She's right, I know that for sure. I thank her again for the meal, tip her well and head out the door. As I leave, she calls to me and says, "Hey, don't forget, the love, that love I was talking about, that love is here." She waves her arm around in a circle over her head, "it's all around us." I smile, thank her again and walk out the door shaking my head. What does she mean?

I get back in the car and pull out of the driveway, a car races by me in the left lane...I follow slowly behind. Here we go.

Welcome to DAY 1.

So glad you're on this journey with us.

Today we're talking about Love. Take a minute and watch the lyric video to the song "Love Is Here" on Youtube. It's the first single and the first song on the album. It was actually one of the last songs I wrote for the album. I remember meeting Scotty, my producer, on the first day of the sessions back in November 2016. We sat downstairs in his studio and he said, "Ok, whatcha got?" I played him this song, he smiled, looked at me and said, "we're starting with that one."

He took it to a place that i never thought possible. I'm so happy with the way this song came out, the message, the production, all of it. I hope you enjoy it as much as I do, it's easily one of my favorite tunes on the record.

LOVE IS HERE (Pettigrew) © 2017 Zoovid Music

Love walks into my house and turns the lights back on
Love walks into my doubt when trust is all but gone
Love runs into my heart and tears the finish line
Love runs into my scars and heals them everytime, everytime

AND LOVE IS BURNING THROUGH MY VEINS
IT'S ALL THAT WILL REMAIN
IT'S HERE AND LOVE IS NOW
AND LOVE IS ALL I WANNA KNOW
IT'S THE PROMISE THAT I HOLD WHEN MY DREAMS DISAPPEAR
AND LOVE IS HERE

Love sees every answer and all that hides beneath
Love makes me a dancer when I can't feel the beat
Love leads my soul so far to worlds I'd never find
Love is brighter than the stars and love is kind

AND LOVE IS BURNING THROUGH MY VEINS
IT'S ALL THAT WILL REMAIN
IT'S HERE AND LOVE IS NOW
AND LOVE IS OUT OF MY CONTROL
IT'S THE SUNSHINE AND THE SNOW IT WILL HOLD ON THROUGH THE YEARS
AND LOVE IS HERE

Love is hanging there saying I have died for you
Love is giving life so that you can make it through
Love is loving more so that you can win your war
Love is what your heart has been longing for
It's all that will remain, it's here and love is now

AND LOVE IS BURNING THROUGH MY VEINS
IT'S ALL THAT WILL REMAIN
IT'S HERE AND LOVE IS NOW
AND LOVE WILL NEVER LET YOU GO
IT WILL ALWAYS HOLD YOU CLOSE AND YOU DON'T HAVE TO FEAR
'CAUSE LOVE IS HERE

4

Love Is Here.

"Love walks into my house and turns the lights back on." So many verses on love in the Bible, so many ideas about what it is, how it works, how Jesus is the author of love. The perfect example of love. Here are some of my favorite verses that speak about love:

Psalm 89:1 – I will sing of the Lord's unfailing love forever. Young and old will hear of your faithfulness.

Romans 8:38 – And I am convinced that nothing can separate us from God's love. Neither death nor life, neither angels nor demons, neither our fears for today nor our worries about tomorrow, not even the powers of hell can separate us from God's love.

John 3:16 – For this is how God loved the world: He gave his one and only Son, so that everyone who believes in Him will not perish but have eternal life.

Love is inexplicable. It is unpredictable. It's beautiful. It's painful. Sometimes it hurts but love conquers all. Every time.

"Love Is Here" is a song that was healing for me. I wrote it at the end of 2016. Little did I know that 6 months later I'd be singing it in a studio in Atlanta letting the words sink into my soul and heal me. You see, on Good Friday in April of 2017 my nephew Ryan died of an accidental heroin overdose in the basement of my home. In response to that event we as a family had two choices. One was to let the grief overcome us. The other was to let love overcome us. We chose the latter. The outpouring of love that we felt was incredible. The true love of Jesus pouring into our lives from His children. People surrounded us, held us close and wrapped their arms around us. Sat with us, prayed with us, listened. We watched and experienced this unpredictable, wonderful, strong, inexplicable, bright and beautiful love that Jesus gives us invade our lives.

Our grief continues but we rest in the love that Jesus brought to us during that time and continues to give us. As I wrote this song I liked to look back on the lyric and replace the word love in every line with the name Jesus. It makes for an interesting prayer and meditation tactic. Try it.

Jesus walks into my house and turns the lights back on.
Jesus walks into my doubt when trust is all but gone.
Jesus runs into my heart and tears the finish line.
Jesus runs into my scars and heals them every time.

Today. Take time to let Jesus run into your heart. Let Him heal you.

PRAYER: God. Today, we long for your love in our lives. We all hurt, we all have pain, but today we pray that Your love would work deeply in our hearts. Restore us. Heal us. Let the love of Jesus pull us deeper into a trusting relationship with You.

Chapter 2
UNDERTOW

CHAPTER 2:
Undertow

It wasn't long before the rain started. Long streams of it pushing against the windshield as I drive. I think secretly I was hoping that I'd have to turn back. You see, when you face something really difficult, you get scared. You don't want it to happen. You just want it to go away. Well that's not happening here. There's no going back. My mind wanders as my car coasts along this mirror of a highway. I think of better times, times when we were together. I miss her so much, I'm not sure what happened. That's what part of this is about. Is there redemption? Is there a way to regain what was lost?

The highway leads me around a bend and a sharp corner opens up to the ocean on my right hand side and a mountain on my left. I can see past the guardrail, the waves crash up against the stones. Waves crash into the crevices and jet the water into the air. I've always loved the ocean. I've always loved the sound of the waves. My life has turned into this stormy sea. The business, the work, the responsibility, all played a part in where I am today. My palms get sweaty as i remember all the late nights, all the birthday parties missed, the arguments, the words that I wish could be thrown into this ocean on my right and drowned. Wouldn't it be nice to just let the undertow pull them out and let them never be heard again. Too easy. Life doesn't work that way. A word spoken is out there. My father always told me to choose my words carefully, to think before speaking. The time lost can't be reclaimed. The fractures in a relationship, they are hard to heal.

I can feel the wheels slide underneath me as the car begins the drift. There's something about hydroplaning that leaves you feeling hopeless. That feeling matches my emotions right now. As i drift to the left, the oncoming truck in the other lane lays on his horn.....

Welcome to DAY 2.

Thanks for stopping back in. Great to see you again.

Today we're talking about letting go. About how God never lets go. This song is all about our capacity to excel in the struggle. How we so quickly get wrapped up in our own messes. How we get caught up in the waves of life and how God never ever lets go. How He reaches down below the surface and draws us back to Him. Every day. All the time.

I remember writing this song and really loving the idea of getting caught in the Undertow of God's grace. I was born and raised around the ocean and love nautical themes, sea stories, lighthouses, etc. The imagery in this song was born right out of my childhood growing up on the beach. So many of these themes I now look at and use in my relationship with God. Getting caught in the Undertow and having Him pull me up. Drawing me close.

I love the second verse of this song, I love the imagery of the fog and through it Jesus walking to meet us. So powerful. What's the fog hiding in your life?

I remember as we recorded this we were looking for different things to make different noises. We were in a studio in Georgia, nowhere near the ocean. So we used other things to make the sounds we needed. At one point in the session, Scotty pulls a folding lawn chair out of the closet and grabs a mic. I'm shaking my head, wondering what is happening. He starts playing the chair on 2 and 4, with the drums! It sounded great! Don't believe me, watch the video in the journey links! It added this slap to the track that we didn't have before. The waves that you hear in this track are being created by blowing air through a Kazoo, then soaked in reverb & delay. I will never doubt him again :) . This was a fun session. The track has so much going on and then we had these great gang vocals at the end. Such a great time recording this one.

I hope you enjoy listening to it as much as we did writing and recording it.

I'm breathing in, I'm breathing out
I'm fighting through the fear and doubt
I lift my hands I lift my heart
I'm drowning in your grace.....

UNDERTOW (Pettigrew/Wilbanks) © 2017 Zoovid Music,

the water's dark the water's deep, the water's crashing over me
my cries are washed up on the beach, and no one hears a sound
I take a breath, I breathe you in, I take a step but can't begin
'cause I'm still caught in this headwind, this ship has run aground

I'M GETTING CAUGHT IN THE UNDERTOW
GETTING PULLED DOWN BY THE WAVES
TAKE MY HAND NOW AND PULL ME CLOSE
I'M GOING DOWN TODAY
I'M GETTING CAUGHT IN THE UNDERTOW
THE DARKNESS PULLING AT MY FEET
BUT YOU ARE HERE RIGHT NOW I KNOW
AND YOU'RE NOT LETTING GO

a flicker of light a flicker of hope, a star that shines from a distant coast
and through the fog He looks like a ghost, but He calms the storms in me
I walk on water, I walk through fear, my faith is strong when it appears
but there's no room for doubting here in the midst of these high seas

CHORUS:

I'm breathing in I'm breathing out, I'm fighting through the fear and doubt
I lift my hands, I lift my heart, I'm drowning in Your grace
Your love is washing over me, I'm finally home, I'm finally free
I'm reaching up, You're reaching down, I'm drowning in your grace

I'M GETTING CAUGHT IN THE UNDERTOW
GETTING PULLED DOWN BY THE WAVES
TAKE MY HAND NOW AND PULL ME CLOSE
I'M GOING DOWN TODAY
I'M GETTING CAUGHT IN THE UNDERTOW
THE DARKNESS PULLING AT MY FEET
YOU ARE HERE RIGHT NOW I KNOW
AND YOU'RE NOT LETTING GO

Undertow.

"The water's dark, the water's deep, the water's crashing over me."

Life. It's hard. I heard someone say years ago that sometimes you just feel like saying, "Stop the world and let me off." Do you feel like that today? Do you feel the water rising?

Daily, the onslaught of new information, advertising, texts, emails and more force their way into our lives. We are overwhelmed. This means that it's that much more important to take time each day to step back, take a breath. It's hard, we are pulled in so many directions. The pull is strong, the undertow of life drags us down.

A few verses to rest in:

Psalm 46:10 – "Be still and know that I am God."

John 16: 23 – "I have told you all this so that you may have peace in me. Here on earth you will have many trials and sorrows. But take heart, because I have overcome the world."

Undertow - another term for rip current, it's the average under-current which moves offshore when waves are approaching a shore.

Every day we are pulled. Pulled away from a relationship with our God. Work, play, entertainment. So many things distract us. We get caught in the undertow of life daily. I remember years ago getting caught in the undertow of an addiction to work, not being able to stop. The pull of wanting more, Wanting to have more. It's powerful. This life entices us, draws us into it. Jesus tells us in John that we are not of this world. **John 15:19 says this, "The world would love you as one of its own if you belonged to it, but you are no longer part of this world. I chose you to come out of the world, so it hates you."**

The pull of this world is strong. It takes a conscious effort every day to find time to spend with God. To be still with Him. To rest in Him. Today, be sure to take a few moments. Put the phone down, look away from the screen, take a break at work and just...rest. Rest in Your Savior. Rest in this God who loves you so very much. Let Him heal you, let Him restore you. Take time daily to sit at His feet and learn from Him. Be made strong in Him.

The undertow of life is so easy to get pulled into. Fight it.

PRAYER: God, today, so many things are pulling me in. You are my one true source of hope and life. I pray that I would be made strong through the time that I spend with You. Restore me. Fill me with your grace, Your love, Your hope. Let me be pulled free from the undertow of life and rest in the undertow of your love & grace today.

Chapter 3
FAITH AND GASOLINE

CHAPTER 3:
Faith And Gasoline

The feeling of losing control is terrifying. When we lose control of a relationship, a situation, our thoughts. There's nothing quite like it. Right now. I've lost control. I'm in this desperate feeling of in between.

Everything slowed down as my hands gripped and cranked the wheel to the right, away from the truck, our mirrors collided like two waves crashing into each other, glass shattered and cracked. The mirror was torn from my car like a leaf gets blown from a tree in autumn, an easy break. My car slides to a halt and the truck swerves into the breakdown lane on the other side. The driver clamors out of the truck, "You OK?", he calls out. "Yeah," I respond,. I think my pride was hurt more than anything else. "What happened?" he asked. What did happen, where was I? Did I remember that I was actually driving a two ton ball of metal at sixty miles an hour? I shook my head, "I'm sorry, I'm in the middle of something and just drifted into the other lane." I wiped the rain from my face and looked into his eyes. The adrenaline slowing down in both our bodies. "OK," he said. "Well, is there anything I can do?" I look out at the water, a boat slowly drifts between the waves, it seems lost at sea. "I don't think so." I reply. "This is something I need to take care of myself." "Stay safe and please be careful." He says, and walks away giving me a wave. "Don't worry about the mirror, it's on me this time." I think of the waitress at the diner, her goodness. I think of this truck driver, his goodness, kindness.

The rain stops, the darkness of the storm cracks with the sun shining through a sliver in the clouds. Sometimes we need to break something in order to get back on the right road. To snap us back into place. Make us see things from a different perspective. Before I get back in the car, I wait. I think. I hear a small voice calling out to me. It's my sons voice. He's 4 years old again and he's smiling, holding my hand and looking up into my eyes. I'm his father, no one else in the world compares to me at this moment in his life. That was so many years ago. I shake my head and wipe a tear from my eye. I miss those days. I miss those moments when we were together. There has to be a way to right this wrong. There has to. I get back into the car and start the engine and shift into gear....

Welcome to DAY 3.

We're all settling into this together. So good that you're here. Thanks.

Today we're talking about the journey. The road we're on. How even when it's dark and lonely God is still there. Even when it's sunny, God is there. Everything in between. God is there. Buckle up today. Be ready for anything. God is with you today on the journey. Keep your eyes and ears open for Him as He speaks to you today.

This song has such an interesting vibe to it. We tried to make it literally sound like the inside of a car as you're driving down the highway. There are some percussive elements that lend to the lines in a road, the bumps, the cracks. It cruises along through the first and second verses & choruses and then we get to this breakdown. This is where the road opens up, where we hit cruise control as we have this epiphany. "Finally I see the darkness crack with the dawn, finally." It's about new beginnings, about new ideas. We end the bridge by shifting into another gear and letting the guitar just rip out a solo. I love this song, really love it. The imagery, the vibe, all of it. People have asked why I called the album Faith And Gasoline. It's all about our faith in God. How every day I try to walk by faith. Some days I fail miserably, others, I see it. I see the goodness of God in everything. Those are the days I long for. The gasoline in the title is literally the gas that we put in our cars to get from one gig to the next. God provides. He's walking with us every step of the way.

Today, as you continue your journey, continue to seek God. Look for Him in all of it.

Hope you enjoy this one as much as I do.

Finally
I'm shifting to another gear
Finally...
Finally...

Faith & Gasoline (Pettigrew/Di Minno/Wilbanks) © 2017 Zoovid Music, Turn It Up Productions

it's lonely here tonight, it's me and the white lines flashing by
i'm just a ball of light, searching for home
ahead i see the red lights shine, there's no way they'll slow me down
i'm looking for an exit sign, and a place to call home

THERE'S NO STOPPING ME NOW, I'M JUST LOST IN THE HOW
AND THIS FEELING OF IN BETWEEN
BUT I'LL GO WHERE YOU LEAD AND MAYBE ALL THAT I NEED
IS A LITTLE FAITH AND GASOLINE

the gaslight's shining bright, i'm drifting to the other lane
i'll roll on through the night, into the unknown

THERE'S NO STOPPING ME NOW, I'M JUST LOST IN THE HOW
AND THIS FEELING OF IN BETWEEN
BUT I'LL GO WHERE YOU LEAD AND MAYBE ALL THAT I NEED
IS A LITTLE FAITH AND GASOLINE

and finally, i see the darkness crack with the dawn, finally...
and finally, there's hope i've never seen before, finally...
and finally, i feel like i am finally here, finally...
and finally, i'm shifting to another gear, finally, finally...

THERE'S NO STOPPING ME NOW, I'M JUST LOST IN THE HOW
AND THIS FEELING OF IN BETWEEN
BUT I'LL GO WHERE YOU LEAD AND MAYBE ALL THAT I NEED
IS A LITTLE FAITH AND GASOLINE
A LITTLE FAITH AND GASOLINE

Faith And Gasoline.

And finally, I see the darkness crack with the dawn, finally...
And finally, there's hope I've never seen before, finally...

How often do we feel like this? Finally, the darkness cracks with the dawn. Finally, the long night is over, the sickness is healed, the hurt is gone. God has moved. All of us, I think, at some point feel this way.

We long for answers, we long for God to intervene. We long for the night to be over. This song is about the journey. Life is a journey, there's no way around it. There are mountains to climb, there are deserts to cross, there are storms to weather. These roads we take, Jesus drives with us. Yes, sometimes we feel as though we are stuck with this incredible feeling of in between. He is with us always on every road. A few verses to cling to when the road is dark, when the gaslight is shining bright:

Joshua 1:9 – "Have I not commanded you? Be strong and courageous. Do not be frightened, and do not be dismayed, for the Lord your God is with you wherever you go.

Proverbs 3: 5-6 – "Trust in the Lord with all your heart and lean not on your own understanding, in all your ways acknowledge Him and He will keep your paths straight."

As we get older, we get a more birds eye view of how God has moved in our lives. I can look back on the years and see when I met my wife, how God's hand was there. When I've changed jobs, how God's hand was there. In relationships that I've made, in musicians that I've met. God's hand has been in it all, He has a plan for us. Our job is to maintain a faithful walk with Him. To daily reach deep into His word and put these verses that we learn from childhood into practice. If I had to go back and do it again, I would have leaned more on Jesus in my earlier years. Leaned more on the words that I was taught way back when I was a kid. I would have grown deeper in my walk with Jesus. Now that I'm a little older, I'm playing catch up. I've seen His hand work through it all. I've seen how He moves in and around my life. I see how He has protected, provided, loved and guided.

Today, as you read and pray. Take a minute and look back over the years that you've been walking with Him and see how He's moved. How He's been there all along. The road is dark, yes, the road is long, yes. We walk by faith. We let His hand guide us. Seek Him, watch as the darkness cracks with the dawn, watch as hope is found.

PRAYER: God, today, we lift up our hands to you in thankfulness. Our hearts continuously wander. Our minds shift focus. Our eyes are turned away. Today, we refocus all of it to You. We refocus all of it to your hand of provision, guidance and love. We thank you for all of it. Lead us.

Chapter 4
WHY WON'T YOU LOVE ME

CHAPTER 4:
Why Won't You Love Me

There's comes a point in a long drive where you settle in, you realize that there's no stopping the drive and you get comfortable and let the car do the work. Defenses down. Your mind starts to wander. I was very conscious of the drive since the incident with the truck but at about 250 miles in, i started to get comfortable and started to let my mind relax a little.

Years ago, when we were first married, i remember how everything was so focused on us. On the two of us. Her name is Sarah, she meant and still means the world to me. Our journey is on two different roads right now and this trip is hopefully going to allow them to intersect. I remember a few years in, we started to drift. Actually, I started to drift. She was never the problem here. My work really took a toll on things and I started drifting. I started loving work more than loving our time together. I was never unfaithful but I started taking advantage of her and the fact that she'd always be there.

I remember one evening, after a long argument she just ended the conversation by saying "Why, Tom, why won't you love me like I love you. I feel like I'm second to everything". She was right. I was addicted to work. I was addicted to the rush of closing a deal, the sounds of the office, the fine dinners, the trips, all of it. I was addicted to it and didn't even see the floor falling out below me.

She left, just 3 months ago, took our two beautiful kids and told me it was time for a change. We still talk on the phone but her move to Arizona has changed things. I stupidly let her go, not that I had a choice. I told her I just needed to finish a few things here in New York and then I would join them. One week turned to four, four to eight and the road between us kept getting longer and longer.

I continue on I70 towards St. Louis. The car is pulling to the right, trying to pull me off the road. I suddenly hear what sounds like a gunshot and feel the wheel jerk hard to the right, a harsh flapping sound fills my head and i swerve into the breakdown lane. I jump out. A complete blow out. The tire. My life. The irony in all of it. I hear thunder again in the distance. "Great".

Welcome to DAY 4.

Today we're talking about love again. Where that love comes from. How much God truly loves us. We get so wrapped up in the day to day that we forget that He sent His Son to die for us. For you. For me. Don't forget that today. Jesus came to, for once and for all, conquer death. To show us the true meaning of love.

When we were recording this one we wanted it to get soulful, to feel like a timeless, old soul ballad with the singer just pleading for his life that his love would come back to him. Scotty started playing that great piano intro and everything just kind of fell into place. We got to the end and i said, hey, let's bring it all back again. So, you get that great outro chorus with the choir. So so good. I loved having the choir there. They sang on this song, Don't Give Up On Me and There Is Hope. Such amazing singers! Harmonies, everything, just incredible.

Hope you love this one!

I raise my voice like thunder
try to wake you
from your slumber
It's patient words
I whisper in the wind...

Why Won't You Love Me (Pettigrew/Wilbanks) © 2017 Zoovid Music, Turn It Up Productions

you don't look me in the eyes
you barely hear my voice
i don't know if you'd say you knew me
if you were given the choice
but i'm waiting here alone, i won't be refused
just give me a little hint, that maybe i matter to you
i've tried to show you all i am
i've given you every reason to take my hand

WHY WON'T YOU LOVE ME, WHY WON'T YOU LOVE ME
WHY WON'T YOU LOVE ME LIKE I LOVE YOU

i'm looking for a sign
the competition's fierce
just a little word or two
is all i want to hear
i've given you all i have
yeah i've given you my life
but still you look right through me
like a shadow in the night

CHORUS:

i raise my voice like thunder try to wake you from your slumber
it's patient words i whisper in the wind
there's nothing i wouldn't do to make you feel the love i have for you
so i ask you once again, why won't you love me

WHY WON'T YOU LOVE ME, WHY WON'T YOU LOVE ME
WHY WON'T YOU LOVE ME LIKE I LOVE YOU

WHY WON'T YOU LOVE ME LIKE THE SUN LOVES THE SKY
LIKE TODAY LOVES TONIGHT
WHY WON'T YOU LOVE ME LIKE I LOVE YOU

Why Won't You Love Me.

Sometimes I think of what it must be like for God to be up there, looking down on His creation and wondering, if I love them so much, why don't they love me back? Why can't so many of them see me? Why won't they love me the way that I love them?

It's ridiculous to think this way because God, in His grace and love, doesn't think like this. He thinks in ways that we can't even begin to understand. Our human-ness shines through when we have thoughts like this. He is sovereign. His love exceeds anything we could ever imagine. Yet we, in our small mindedness come to these conclusions. We get caught up in our own guilt. We sometimes fall into the traps set for us every day. Why should God love me? Why should God care? I am a sinner, I sin daily. I fall down every day. If this is you, and it's me quite often, here are a few scriptures to rest in today:

John 15:13 - "Greater love has no one than this: to lay down one's life for one's friends"

Psalm 86:15 - "But you, O Lord, are a compassionate and gracious God, slow to anger, abounding in love and faithfulness."

1 John 4: 7-8 - "Dear friends, let us love one another, for love comes from God. Everyone who loves has been born of God and knows God. Whoever does not love does not know God, because God is love."

This love. This amazing love that Jesus pours out on us every day, is never ending and always there. I can only equate it to the love of a mother or father to their new born baby. I remember when both of my kids were born, there was something that just took over. There was something that opened in my soul. Something that had been dormant for my entire life until those children came into this world. There was a new level of love that existed in my heart. This, I think, is what God is feeling every day towards all of His children. Towards us. He regularly is saying, "I'm here, I love you, I want to be with you, you amaze me".

If you're not feeling it. Let me encourage you. Read those Bible verses above again. Jesus loved us so much that He died for us, His friends. You are a friend of Jesus, a friend of God. When God looks at you, He sees a forgiven, beautiful, wonderful person. God is compassionate, gracious, He abounds in love and faithfulness. Always showing concern for us. Always wanting the best for us. Always the example of love. We all naturally feel inclined to love because He first loved us. He was the example of love to each one of us. God is love. Let that love overwhelm you today. Rest in that love today. Know that you are loved today.

PRAYER: God, sometimes we get so wrapped up in our own emotions, in our own interests that we forget how much You love us. Help us today to remember that You are the author of love. The ultimate example of love. Thank you for Jesus. Thank you for the sacrifice you made. Yours is a perfect and unconditional love.

I've given you all I have
I've given you my life

Chapter 5
FEAR NOT

CHAPTER 5:
Fear Not.

I open the trunk. The spare tire isn't there. Amazing. Now what. I look down at my phone, no service. To the left and right there's highway and a lot of it. I start walking. I think I saw a town a few miles back. Thirty minutes into the walk I see a small church over a hill. I make my way towards it. It looks abandoned. A parsonage sits on the left side and there's a car in the driveway. I make my way over, up the porch and knock on the door. A small man, probably 5' 2" opens it. Gray hair and lines on his face that could write a book.

"Can I help ya," he says. I tell him my story and he smiles. "Happens about two or three times a month" he says, "there's a gas station a few miles down the road, I can give you a lift but I've got lunch on the table. Join me and then we can go. My name's Paul by the way"

I walk into the house. Typical colonial with the staircase on the right just inside the door heading up to the second floor. I stop and look at the history that climbs the wall up these stairs. Pictures hang. Memories trapped in frames that tell the story of this man's life.

"Those are my kids, my wife, even my two dogs are up there." He chuckles. "They were my best friends a lot of the time".

"Where is everyone now?" I ask. "Oh, they're all gone." He shuffles his feet. "My wife passed on a few years back and my kids are in California and Alaska. I used to pastor that church there but everything's kind of dried up around here and I'm finding it hard to find a congregation." He smiles again, a warm smile. The kind of smile that says I'm here to help and I'm here to listen.

We head into the dining room and sit down. Grilled cheese and ham sandwiches and two Cokes sit on the table. In the center is a single daisy in a vase. He sees me staring at it. "Those were Emma's favorite. She loved daisies." I thank him for the food and he says grace. Thanks God for all of it, the food, the house, the family, everything.

"How can you still have faith after all this time? You're here alone, your kids have left and your wife is gone and yet you still hold onto your faith. Isn't that hard? Aren't you lonely? Scared?" He takes a bite and a sip and I watch his eyes meet mine. "For years I had all that you saw on that staircase. I had a woman whom I loved. I have two amazing kids who still check in from time to time which I'm grateful for. But most of all I have a trust and friendship in a God who loves me unconditionally. I'm seventy two years old. I've seen Him in the good and the bad. I've seen Him fight for me and I've seen Him deliver me. My family. I loved my wife until the day she died. The last words that she said to me were, "fear not, i'm with you now and forevermore, I love you." Then she kissed my cheek and slipped away."

I apologized. He said, "No need to apologize. It's life. I'm just really thankful for the time that I had with her. Just over 50 years. Pretty amazing." I see his eyes tear a little. "So tell me your story. What brings you out on this highway?"

"Well, there's a lot to it", I say. So I tell him everything. For some reason I felt safe with him. Comfortable. He's been a pastor all his life and I'm sure he's heard everything but he listens to my story as if it was the first time he's ever heard it. I finish by saying that I'm on my way out to Arizona to see the kids but also try and turn this around. "I have to turn this around. I still love her."

The lightning crashes outside and the lights flicker. The rain comes down in sheets. Paul heads over to the window to close it before the rain sneaks into the house. "Looks like you'll be here for a minute." He says.

Welcome to DAY 5.

Fear not. I am with you. Sometimes we just need to hear that. Sometimes, somedays, it's hard to get out of bed because we're afraid of what the day will bring. Today, listen, hear Jesus saying, fear not, I am with you. Fear not, I'm by your side. Fear not.

This was a late night session. I think we started this one at around midnight. We had this lyric, the melody and the chord changes but needed a hook. As you can hear in the original demo, we changed alot of the chorus on this one. Scotty started playing this beautiful two note intro over the changes that we had and I started singing over it. It just took shape. I wish I had recorded that night. The way it came together was really magical. We knew that we had something special. Simple. Something that reflected the love of a father to a child.

We also knew that this was a song that needed strings. Scotty took the tracks up to Nashville and a guy named David Davidsen arranged them and played with a quartet. I absolutely LOVE the way this one came out. Tender, sweet. The message is spot on and exactly what I had envisioned for this one from the very beginning when I wrote it in my attic.

Enjoy this and feel the presence of your heavenly Father holding you close. Urging you to fear not. He's here.

Fear Not (Pettigrew/Wilbanks) © 2017 Zoovid Music, Turn It Up Productions

i conquer the wind, i conquer the waves
i move mountains, when there's no other way
i give hope, when there's no hope to find
give healing to the broken sight to the blind

FEAR NOT, I AM WITH YOU
FEAR NOT, I'M BY YOUR SIDE
FEAR NOT, I'LL HOLD YOU TONIGHT
FEAR NOT

i am your shield when life tears you down
when you walk through the valley, through the battleground
i am the light on the darkened road
i give you all that I am, your cup overflows

FEAR NOT, I AM WITH YOU
FEAR NOT, I'M BY YOUR SIDE
FEAR NOT, I'LL HOLD YOU TONIGHT
FEAR NOT

and i'll hold you forever
'cause that's what daddy's do
and i'll be here forever, i will always love you

FEAR NOT, I AM WITH YOU
FEAR NOT, I'M BY YOUR SIDE
FEAR NOT, I'LL HOLD YOU TONIGHT
FEAR NOT

Fear Not.

I conquer the winds, I conquer the waves.
I move mountains, when there's no other way.

Fear. It consumes us some days. It overcomes us other days. Some mornings even getting out of bed doesn't come easy because of our fear of what the day may bring. Jesus teaches us that we need not be afraid. His peace is with us. His peace, which transcends all understanding, walks with us daily. A few verses to ponder on what the Bible says about fear:

John 14:27 – "Peace I leave with you, my peace I give to you. I do not give to you as the world gives. Do not let your hearts be troubled and do not be afraid."

Matthew 6:34 – "Therefore, do not worry about tomorrow, for tomorrow will worry about itself. Each day has enough trouble of its own.

Psalm 23:4 – "Even though I walk through the darkest valley, I will fear no evil, for you are with me; your rod and your staff, they comfort me.

Psalm 34:4 – "I sought the Lord and he answered me, he delivered me from all my fears."

The list goes on and on. Actually, fear is spoken of in over 500 verses in the Bible and "fear not" is the most repeated command in the Bible. Incredible.

The bridge of this song brings home the reality of the love of the Father.

"And I'll hold you forever, 'cause that's what Daddy's do, I'll be here forever, I will always love you." God holds us. He is our loving Father, our Abba. Our Father watching over us each and every day. How He loves us and how He longs to hold us in His arms and comfort us. Rest in that today. Let the strength of God hold you in His arms today. Fear not, He is with us. Fear not, He's by our side.

What are you afraid of today? Surrender it to God. What is holding you back today? Surrender that to God. Take comfort in the arms of Jesus wrapped around you as you walk through your day. Fear, anxiety, stress. All of these keep us from a trusting relationship with Jesus. Pray for peace. Take a breath, hold it, then release it. Let your meditations today be on the peace of the Lord. Let your heart rest in Him.

PRAYER: God today, hold me, let Your spirit of peace surround me in the midst of my fear and anxiety. Relieve the stress that I feel. Let my thoughts point me back to you as I go through my day. Let the words of my mouth and the meditations of my heart be acceptable to You Lord. Draw me near to You.

Chapter 6
ME

CHAPTER 6.
Me.

It was more than a minute. The storm raged on for hours, through the night. The power went out, a tree fell outside and severed the line. Paul said that this one of the worst storms he'd seen in years. He was kind, made up a bed for me. Actually said he was happy to have the company. We sat by the fire and talked till late into the night. I learned about his family, his wife, his kids. All of it. He had led quite a life. Content the whole way through, leaning on God through it all. He gave me hope. He had a way with words, a way with advice and knowledge that I admired.

He told me that patience was the key. We are all so very anxious to get to the goal and along the way we miss the journey. It's all about the journey. That's where the meat is. Life is the journey. It's not the destination.

The more we talk the more I miss my family. I've missed the journey. I know it. As Paul talks I drift off in thought again. His words get clouded and I see this movie in my mind. My kids growing up, my wife laughing, the house, the life that I used to have. I've become someone else, this epiphany brings tears to my eyes.

I'm tired of trying to be someone else. I'm tired of this double life. I confess this to Paul. He gives me a nod and a thumbs up. "That's what it's about Tom. When we get to that point of being honest, real, authentic. We're getting closer to it. What that is is different for every person."

I've been living through these days with blinders on. They've consumed me and all along I've missed the real stuff. The good stuff. I feel like I've hit a wall.

Paul is standing by me, shaking me a little. "Where'd you go Tom," he says. "I'm here," I say. "I'm just wishing that I'd met you about 10 years ago." "It's OK," he says. "You've got time."

The next morning we head out, the sun rays breaking through the clouds seem to point an arrow in the direction I need to go. Paul drives me to my car, we grab the flat tire and head to the gas station. The house mechanic named Jake gives me a deal there and we're back on the road to fix my flat.

As we drive, I glance out the window. The car is silent, I hear the thump in the road as the tires roll. I'm tired. Tired of all this make believe. I want my life back. My real life.

35

Welcome to DAY 6.

Me. I love this song. A little throw back to the eighties. We had fun recording this one. Listened to a bunch of Phil Collins, Duran Duran, Eddie Money, Toto and more before we created the arrangement and recorded it.

The message is simple. We are meant to be so much more than anything we could ever dream of. The world continues to push us in one direction, God pushes us in a very different direction. A direction that speaks of love, hope, truth, honesty, respect, fidelity. Today, as you listen and read below, think about what that means to you. As the chorus of this song says "I wanna be me, not someone else that I'm trying to be." Today, be who God meant for you to be.

I wanna be me not someone else that i m trying to be

Me (Pettigrew/Wilbanks) © 2017 Zoovid Music, Turn It Up Productions

i've been living the nine to five,
caught in the crossfire of wrong and right
okay with the status quo, a little ant marching down this road
i've been chained to this chair and desk
phone wrapped around my neck, the day's a mess
but somewhere deep in my soul, i hear your voice calling me home
calling me home, calling me home to what you've been waiting for

I WANNA BE ME, NOT SOMEONE ELSE THAT I'M TRYING TO BE
I'M TIRED OF ALL THIS MAKE BELIEVE, JUST ME
I WANNA BE REAL, WITH ARMS WIDE OPEN AND EYES THAT SEE
IN THIS BROKEN WORLD WHAT WE REALLY NEED IS ME
TO BE ALL YOU MADE ME TO BE

there's so much more that i can do
what have i got to lose there's no excuse
so hear my when i pray make me someone who saves the day
not a hero so they can cheer
but someone who makes it clear that i'll be here
let me give what matters most, time and love and let me give hope
i wanna know, i wanna know what you have made me for

I WANNA BE ME, NOT SOMEONE ELSE THAT I'M TRYING TO BE
I'M TIRED OF ALL THIS MAKE BELIEVE, JUST ME
I WANNA BE REAL, WITH ARMS WIDE OPEN AND EYES THAT SEE
IN THIS BROKEN WORLD WHAT WE REALLY NEED IS ME
TO BE ALL YOU MADE ME TO BE

BRIDGE:
i'm tired of my wheels spinning 'round
so put my soul back on your ground
it's time to let the old me go
and bring this wanderer home

I WANNA BE ME, NOT SOMEONE ELSE THAT I'M TRYING TO BE
I'M TIRED OF ALL THIS MAKE BELIEVE, JUST ME
I WANNA BE REAL, WITH ARMS WIDE OPEN AND EYES THAT SEE
IN THIS BROKEN WORLD WHAT WE REALLY NEED IS ME
TO BE ALL YOU MADE ME TO BE

Me.

I wanna be me. Not someone else that I'm trying to be.

Today. Think about how many advertisements you'll see. The average American is exposed to between 4,000 and 10,000 ads per day. It's nauseating. All of these ads telling us who we should be, what makes us better, how our lives can be better. They tell us what we should be wearing, eating, driving. Ads tell us that we'll be better if we have this or that. If we upgrade to the newest "it" phone or device.

Jesus tells us it's not about that. It's not about what the world can give us but what He can give us.

John 14:6 - Jesus answered, "I am the way and the truth and the life. No one comes to the Father except through me.

Romans 12:2 - Do not be conformed to this world, but be transformed by the renewal of your mind, that by testing you may discern what is the will of God, what is good and acceptable and perfect.

1 John 2:15 - 17 - Do not love the world or the things in the world. If anyone loves the world, the love of the Father is not in him. For all that is in the world—the desires of the flesh and the desires of the eyes and pride in possessions—is not from the Father but is from the world. And the world is passing away along with its desires, but whoever does the will of God abides forever.

These verses cut deep sometimes. It's hard. We live in the world, we are surrounded by the world. When I wrote this song I was tired of the constant bombardment of "the world" in everyday life. Tired of people that I don't even know trying to tell me who I should be. It's exhausting trying to be someone else. It's exhausting trying to live two different lives. The idea of this song is to take all that we are, all that Jesus gives us and put it into practice. To take the truth, the love, the hope that Jesus gives and make it part of our everyday lives.

It's so easy to get wrapped up in the world. In the temptations and materialism of it all. Jesus is calling us to be the "me" that we're supposed to be. The people He made us to be. His children, His ambassadors here on earth. Spreading His love, His hope, His goodness, His grace, His mercy, His kindness. Where does that fit into everyday life and what we see in Hollywood, in TV, in advertising? It normally doesn't. We are meant for more. We are here for more. Today, be the person that God made you to be. Be the me you were meant to be.

PRAYER: God, today, let me see the me that you made me to be. Let me be the me that you made me to be. Let me be Jesus in the world. Let me be His hands, His feet. Let me set aside the temptations of the world and focus on You. Keep my eyes focused on You. Keep my heart focused on You so that I can be drawn closer to You.

There's so much more
that i could do
What have I got lose
there's no excuse...

Chapter 7
REFLECTION OF YOU

CHAPTER 7.
Reflection of You.

I give Paul a hug as I get ready to leave. He smiles, pats me on the back and says, "Go. Go and make amends. Go and be the father you were meant to be. The man you were meant to be. The man God made you to be. We're all a reflection of Him. Especially as a father. Be a reflection of Him and seek Him more. Find Him in your kids, in your wife. In the relationships that you're going to rebuild."

I can tell he's preaching now but I humor him. This is what he was put on this earth to do. Guide others. Lead others. Show others "The Way." I thank him again and get in the car.

The miles are drifting away behind me, the road ahead once again seems long. I see the horizon in the distance and can't help but feel a new sense of purpose. Something new is driving me now.

Paul talked a lot about his relationship with God last night and this morning. I'd always known about God but never really focused my attention on living a life that reflected who He was. Paul spoke the night before about how being a follower of God meant that things were different. Goals were different and agendas were different. How the things we do are not to bring us fame but to bring Him fame. To show others His goodness and be a reflection of Him here on earth. I listened. Intently. I liked what I heard and felt something inside me change as we prayed together. He brought me back. I could see the light shining inside and out. This night changed me. This night changed everything.

I caught my reflection in the gas station window as I stopped to fill the tank. I looked different. I felt different. I felt changed. I felt thankful. This weight, this burden of all of it was just lifted off my shoulders. I smiled at the reflection and for the first time in while, felt new.

I lifted the receiver and dropped a quarter in the phone on the wall. Dialed a number and waited. After three rings, Sarah's voice answered. "Hello?"

Welcome to DAY 7.

Relection of You. All that we do, God let it be a reflection of You.

This song, I remember, was recorded, or at least started, at a very late night session. Scotty had come up with the great opening piano line that we loved, then we just went from there. This song is one of my favorites on the album. I love the message, how it's presented and the groove. It was the last song that we finished on the album. I remember when we did the lead vocals, I was really hesitant with them. I didn't think I got it. Wasn't sure they were right. I remember sitting on the plane on the flight back and saying to myself, "I'm going to have to come back and re-sing that one. It didn't feel right." Scotty sent me the roughs a few weeks later and man was I wrong! So good. I am so pleased with the way it turned out. Really feels great, it's the closest song to a worship song that we have on the record.

Take time to dig into the devotional on the following pages. The message here is so important, it's why Jesus came here. He came here to teach us how to be a reflection of Him. How to be His hands and feet here on earth. Take time today to be a reflection of Jesus.

Help me to see with Your eyes Hear with Your ears...

Reflection of You (Pettigrew/Wilbanks) © 2017 Zoovid Music, Turn It Up Productions

There are days, when everything seems crazed
when every good intention, does no good at all
and there are times, when i just can't read the signs
and every road i travel, ends at a wall
there is hope in every prayer, i breathe you in and find you there

HELP ME TO SEE WITH YOUR EYES, AND HEAR WITH YOUR EARS
LEAN ON THE LAUGHTER AND TASTE EVERY TEAR
HOLD ON TO NOTHING BUT YOUR PRECIOUS LOVE
AND GIVE ALL THAT I CAN AND NEVER GIVE UP
EVERYTHING THAT I DO, LET IT BE A REFLECTION OF YOU

the words i speak, the right and wrong and what's in between
the times that i give all that i can, and give a little more
i want to be, more of you and less of me
let others see you, in all that I do, your light shining through
let me be your human mirror, everything is getting clearer

HELP ME TO SEE WITH YOUR EYES, AND HEAR WITH YOUR EARS
LEAN ON THE LAUGHTER AND TASTE EVERY TEAR
HOLD ON TO NOTHING BUT YOUR PRECIOUS LOVE
AND GIVE ALL THAT I CAN AND NEVER GIVE UP
EVERYTHING THAT I DO, LET IT BE A REFLECTION OF YOU

i'm letting go, of every part of everything that's ever kept me from believing
now that i know, i want to see the world you see i want to be the change we're
needing

HELP ME TO SEE WITH YOUR EYES, AND HEAR WITH YOUR EARS
LEAN ON THE LAUGHTER AND TASTE EVERY TEAR
HOLD ON TO NOTHING BUT YOUR PRECIOUS LOVE
AND GIVE ALL THAT I CAN AND NEVER GIVE UP
EVERYTHING THAT I DO, LET IT BE A REFLECTION OF YOU

Reflection of You.

I want to be more of You and less of me.
Let others see You, in all that I do, Your light shining through.

Each day. All that we do. The decisions we make. The way we act with our kids. The way we treat our co-workers, our friends, people we don't know. All of it is a reflection of Jesus. All of it.

Jesus calls us to be like Him. To treat others like Him. He gives us this amazing example of how to be....human. A few verses to reflect on with this in mind:

2 Corinthians 5:17 – Therefore if anyone is in Christ, he is a new creation, the old things pass away, behold, new things have come.

1 John 2:6 – The one who says he abides in Him ought to walk in the same manner himself as He walked.

1 Corinthians 11:1 – Be imitators of me, just as I also am of Christ.

Countless times throughout the Bible Jesus calls us to be imitators of Him. To do as He did. To walk as He walked. To love as He loved.

It's so easy each day to slip into our own ways. To slip into old habits that haunt us. Jesus calls us to be like Him. As we get older, it gets harder to change. We need to fight the apathy. Fight the resistance to change and pray continuously that God would open our hearts, our minds and give us the desire to change. We need to soften our hearts and be open to the change that God wants so desperately to bring to us.

Often when I pray, I ask God to change me. To use me for His purpose. To let everything that we do be done for His glory, not for ours. In a world that so desperately needs a Savior, today I encourage you to take time to seek God. Take time to ask for change. Take time to be drawn closer to Him and to be changed by your time together. Take time to be the hands and feet of Jesus. I've heard it said that the more time you spend with someone, the more like them you become. I want to be more like Jesus. I want my life to be a reflection of Him. I want other people to see Him in me. Make this your prayer today.

PRAYER: God. Today. Let my life be a reflection of You. Let my thoughts mirror Your thoughts. Let my ways be Your ways. Let my heart be broken by the things that break your heart and let that bring about a change in me. Change me today to be more like You. I want to be more of You and less of me.

Let it be done. Amen.

Let me be your human mirror everything is getting clearer.

Chapter 8
ON'T GIVE UP ON ME

CHAPTER 8:
Don't Give Up On Me

I freeze. The next five seconds feel like an eternity. My thoughts are racing through my head. Do I hang up? Do I say hello? Do I drop the phone and run? I breath in. Breath out. Then manage to get out, "....Sarah?" She sighs and says, "Hello Tom. What's up?" I say, "Um...I'm in the middle of a long trip out there. Should be there in a few days, do you have time to talk when I get there. I really need to sit down with you and explain a few things. Talk things through." Silence. The kind that makes time stop. Then. "Well, I'm really busy with work and the kids but text me when you get into town and we'll see what we can set up." My heart leaps. "OK." I say. "Sounds great, thank you." She says goodbye and hangs up the phone.

I walk back to the car and get in. Now it will be a game of trying to find the words to say. I just want to ask if we can start over, rewind time. Unfortunately, not that easy. Too many mistakes have been made. I want to be a good man, a better father, a better husband. I just want to say to her I'm here now, can we take the past and push it aside. Don't give up on me. Don't give up on what we have. We can turn this around.

It's easy to say when it's only the windshield listening as I'm driving down the highway. It will be a different story in a few days.

I turn off and find a roadside motel and book a room for the night. I lie on the bed and open the nightstand drawer. In it there's a Bible. I smile and think of Paul. HIs life, his work, his family, his words. I grab the book and open it up. I start with the book of John. It was 9pm when I started reading, I think I fell asleep around 3am. I couldn't stop. This love that this man Jesus exhibited. This unconditional love. The way that he spoke, acted, handled every situation. This is what I've been longing for. This is who I want to be.

There are days in life when things just change. Days that you can pick out of your own life's history where you can say, "That day changed everything." This was one of those days, one of those nights. Things changed that night. Paul's words resonated in my head. His words said surrender. Love. Give hope. Surrender.

So I did. I surrendered it all. My work, my time, my life, my family, my wife. All of it. I couldn't hold onto it anymore. I've been trying to control everything. Little did I know that I needed to surrender all of it first. Then things will start to come together. We as humans get so wrapped up in our own little worlds, thinking everything is about us. It's not. Everything is about others. Serving others. Helping others. Giving others a chance. That's what this is all about.

I wake up the next morning different. I can feel something in my soul that I've never felt before.

Then I hear a knock on the hotel room door.

Welcome to DAY 8.

Thanks for being here.

Today. We're talking about God, never giving up on us. Never letting go. For this song I remember us sitting in a restaurant listening to Wing's "Live & Let Die". Eating ribs and listening to that song just brought on a bunch of ideas for this arrangement. This song has always been a rockin tune but I think we took it to another level on this recording. The message is simple, God never gives up. Ever. I think we give up on Him sometimes, but He never gives up on us. Ever. Today, listening through the song, get wrapped up in the guitars & the horns and the old school-ness of it all but don't miss the message. Don't miss how much God loves you today. No matter what you're struggling with, He's here with us. Never giving up. Never letting go.

You are all i need
So don't give up
on me

Don't Give Up On Me (Pettigrew/Wilbanks) © 2017 Zoovid Music, Turn It Up Productions

I don't have to say that i'm broken
if i didn't say it i'd be wrong
I can feel weight on my shoulders
every day, the same old song
but you say love me and you won't remember
what happened yesterday

OH DON'T GIVE UP ON ME
I'M WAITING FOR MY TIME TO SHINE
AND YOU ARE ALL I NEED
SO DON'T GIVE UP ON ME

there are many mountains i'm climbing
and there are paths i can't find
through the highs and the valleys
You guide my way every time
I know I should hear you, but how can i listen
when i can't get out of my own way

OH DON'T GIVE UP ON ME
I'M WAITING FOR MY TIME TO SHINE
AND YOU ARE ALL I NEED
SO DON'T GIVE UP ON ME

and all i know is who i am but you tell me there's more
here i am stuck in the bottle but you've won the war

OH DON'T GIVE UP ON ME
I'M WAITING FOR MY TIME TO SHINE
AND YOU ARE ALL I NEED
SO DON'T GIVE UP ON ME

Don't Give Up On Me.

All I know is who I am, but You tell me there's so much more.

Sin. It encompasses us daily. Temptation, desire, pride, lust, the list goes on and on. We get so wrapped up in it and the enemy has a field day with our guilt. Our guilt just beats on us day in and day out. We struggle with it so often. I found myself one day just praying, God, don't give up on me. What a foolish prayer. Of course, God will never give up on me but so often I get so wrapped up in my own sin that I feel the need to ask for forgiveness over and over again just to make sure it sticks.

Jesus tells us that we are so much more.

John 1:12 - Yet to all who did receive Him, to those who believed in His name, He gave the right to become children of God.

Romans 6:6 - For we know that our old self was crucified with Him so that the body ruled by sin might be done away with, that we should no longer be slaves to sin.

1 John 3:1 – See what great love the Father has lavished on us, that we should be called children of God! And that is what we are!

Read that last verse again. We are children of God. Not an acquaintance. A child of God. He is our Abba, our loving Father who sent His son to die for us. Please hear me when I say this, God will never give up on you. He will never stop caring about you or loving you. He cares for you as a parent cares for a child. His love knows no bounds. He doesn't care where you've been or what you've done. He so desperately cares about what's next. He's waiting, today, for you to reach out to Him and call on His name. He won't give up on you. There's so much more.

PRAYER: God, today, You call me to You. Help me to not get so wrapped up in my sin that it draws me away from You. Let me realize that I am a sinner and need You every day, every moment. Thank You for never leaving me. Amen.

Chapter 9
THERE IS HOPE
(HOPE IS STILL ALIVE)

Chapter 9:
There Is Hope.

I rub my eyes. I hear it again. I thought it was part of a dream. It wasn't. There's someone outside my door knocking. I look at the clock. It's 6:30am.

I get up, my hair a haystack, my eyes barely focusing and I look through the peephole. It's a guy, probably in his mid twenties. He's looking back and forth and seems really lost. I open the door, the chain still in place. "What's up?" I ask. He gives a sigh of relief. "Oh, sorry, didn't mean to wake you. Um....can you get me some breakfast?" I close my eyes, shake my head, not lost in the randomness of it all and say, "Do I know you?" "No", he answers. "Yours is the seventh door I've knocked on. You're the first to answer."

I think of my night. I think of all that I've been reading. This new person that I'm going to try and be. "OK," I say. "Give me a minute."

I meet him outside in five and we head down to the diner across the street. His name is Darren, he's been on the street for months and can't make ends meet. No family that he remembers. He's alone. He orders pancakes, eggs & bacon. I get a cup of coffee and ask, "What's next for you?" "Not sure," he says, "I think I may try to catch a bus to another city. See what that brings." He rolls his sleeves up before he starts to eat and I can't help but notice the scars. "Hey", I ask. "How long have you been using." "Oh, t his? It's nothing. I've got it under control. A little here and there never hurt anyone." "Yes, it does." I declare, "It hurts everyone. You have to stop." He gets up before he's taken a bite and says, "Thanks for breakfast but I've got to run." "No!" I shout. "Seriously, you need some help. Let me help you."

This is new for me. I've never offered to help a stranger before. Never offered to do much of anything unless I was getting something in return. His eyes look down. "Listen," I say. "I'm rolling through town but I have today. Let me take you somewhere and work on getting you cleaned up. There is hope for you.

He sits down. We talk more. I hear his story. We finish breakfast and I head back to grab my bag from my room. I toss it into my car and give the Bible that was in the nightstand to him. "I just started reading this," I said. "It's changing things." He laughs. "No," I say, "it really is. There's something to it."

I search on my phone for a local recovery group and find one that meets at a church at noon today. Darren and I head out. "What's in it for you," he asks. I shake my head, "Nothing," I answer. "I'm on a bit of a journey right now and this seems to be where I'm supposed to be today. With you. Helping you." I tell him my story, tell him everything.

He listens. It's good to share it again. To talk through it again.

We get to the church and I walk inside with him. Carrie greets us with a warm smile. I introduce myself and let her know that I just met Darren. She's going to bring him inside and have him meet with everyone else. They have rooms at the church. He can stay there. I tell her whatever the cost is, I'll cover it. We exchange information and they walk through the door. Darren turns to me before he goes and says, "Thanks. I don't know why I knocked on your door this morning but sometimes things just happen." "I don't think so, not this time." I reply "We were meant to find each other. God's taking care of both of us on this day. Get clean, go, live and be the man that you're supposed to be. I'll check in on you from time to time and let's stay in touch." He smiles, holds up the Bible that I gave him and waves. He walks through the door into another life.

Welcome to DAY 9.

There is Hope. Today is about hope. It's about the message of hope that Jesus brings. Read the devotional on the next page for a better understanding of the song and what it means to me. It's about hope from addictions. If you think that you're not an addict, think again. We're all in this. You don't have to be addicted to drugs or alcohol to be an addict. You may be addicted to social media, food, pride, porn. I don't know what your addiction is but the point of all of this is to lay that addiction at the feet of Jesus and say, "Father, I can't do this alone and i need Your help." Do that today. Listen to the song, read the devotional below, read the lyrics below & then pray. Pray for hope.

Addicts need love too. Addicts are people too. If you know someone struggling with addiction. First of all, tell them that you love them, give them a hug and then reach out to us. We'll help you find help. Reach out to your local church, they'll help you find help. But...just get help. God has more in store for you then the life you're leading now.

If you're an addict, struggling with an addiction to heroin or any other kind of drug, there's a link on the next page. Reach out to us, we'll help you find someone who can help.

Prayers for all of us as we surrender our addictions to Jesus.

We had a good time recording this one. I loved sharing the story with everyone and letting them know that they are part of something bigger than the song. Bigger than the album. There's a bigger story here and it was amazing to see everyone step up their game as they played their part in the song. Huge thanks to everyone involved. You are all amazing.

Hope you find hope in the midst of your struggle.

There Is Hope (Pettigrew/Di Minno/Wilbanks) © 2017 Zoovid Music, Turn It Up Productions

ten years later i remember blue september skies
i remember how the city streets were so alive
ten years later there are questions that still haunt my mind
answers that are hard to find
places that remind me of you
in this life there are no guarantees

THERE'S A HOPE, THERE'S A FAITH
THERE IS LOVE FOR THE WHOLE HUMAN RACE
THERE'S A HOPE, WE RECEIVE, LET'S US HOLD ON TIGHT TO ALL WE BELIEVE
HOPE NEVER QUITS, HOPE NEVER DIES, HOPE IS STILL ALIVE

ten years later you are still the shelter from the storm
you are still the rock that i have built this house upon
ten years later even though the tears still fall
God you've held me through it all
and i can still call on you
and you alone, are the Savior of us all

THERE'S A HOPE, THERE'S A FAITH
THERE IS LOVE FOR THE WHOLE HUMAN RACE
THERE'S A HOPE, WE RECEIVE, LET'S US HOLD ON TIGHT TO ALL WE BELIEVE
HOPE NEVER QUITS, HOPE NEVER DIES, HOPE IS STILL ALIVE

in our hearts there is a God who will go to any length
and a holy cloud of witnesses who pray to give us strength
the author and perfecter gives us faith to overcome
and on our knees we pray the words, let your will be done

THERE'S A HOPE, THERE'S A FAITH
THERE IS LOVE FOR THE WHOLE HUMAN RACE
THERE'S A HOPE, WE RECEIVE, LET'S US HOLD ON TIGHT TO ALL WE BELIEVE
HOPE NEVER QUITS, HOPE NEVER DIES, HOPE IS STILL ALIVE

Hope is still alive

There. Is. Hope.

In this life, there are no guarantees.

This song. The last song that we recorded for this album, probably means the most on the record. You see, I originally wrote it for the 10th anniversary of September 11th but in the last few years it's turned into a rally cry for those struggling with addictions. Last year, on Good Friday in April 2017, my nephew Ryan died of a accidental heroin overdose in my basement. This changed things. Changed the way I looked at my ministry, at what we were doing and how we were doing it. We decided early on that we were going to use this tragic death for good. We were going to let God use us and use Ryan's life for His glory.

Since then we've started the There Is Hope Movement. We are acting as a conduit between folks who need help from addictions and those who can help. We believe that addiction is a disease, not a character flaw. We believe that addicts are people too. We believe that they need and deserve all the basic human rights that those who aren't struggling with these addictions enjoy. But let's face it, we are all struggling with some type of addiction. You don't have to be struggling with drugs or alcohol to be labelled an addict. You can be struggling with food, pride, social media, porn. Be honest with yourself. You struggle with an addiction. The point of all of this is to lay it all at the feet of Jesus and say, Father, I can't do this alone, I need your help in this. I need you to intervene in my life. I need you to step in here and save me. We need to, all of us, lay our addictions at the foot of the cross and surrender them to Jesus. That's the only way to affect true change. To truly lay them at the feet of Jesus and lean on and rely on His strength through it all.

Now. I understand that recovery from these addictions isn't easy. It's hard. Really hard. When we lost Ryan, I started to dig deeper into the mind of an addict, particularly a heroin addict. This drug just takes over. It changes who you are. Changes your DNA. It's evil. There's no other way to say it.

So, what we're trying to do is, in the name of Jesus, change lives. Because He is the only way, the truth and the life in our own lives. We, as a fallen and broken world, need more of Him in our lives, in our daily walk. We need to push hope, Jesus, deeper into our communities, our schools, our families, our kids. We need to fight for them and fight for who they will become.

John 8:12: Again, Jesus spoke to them, saying, "I am the light of the world. Whoever follows me will not walk in darkness, but will have the light of life."

Galations 2:20 - "I have been crucified with Christ; and it is no longer I who live, but Christ lives in me; and the life which I now live in the flesh I live by faith in the Son of God, who loved me and gave Himself up for me.

Isaiah 64:8 - But now, O LORD, You are our Father, We are the clay, and You our potter; And all of us are the work of Your hand.

These verses are powerful. They mean a lot. They are hard. How do we walk with Jesus? How do we daily pick up our cross and follow Him?

Matthew 16:24 – 26 – "Then Jesus told his disciples, "If anyone would come after me, let him deny himself and take up his cross and follow me. For whoever would save his life will lose it, but whoever loses his life for my sake will find it. For what will it profit a man if he gains the whole world and forfeits his soul? Or what shall a man give in return for his soul?"

This. Is hard. This is where the rubber meets the road as the old saying goes. How do we do this? How is this even possible? Only with Jesus. That's the only way it works. It's a daily walk with Him. Hourly. His ways are not our ways and we are programmed to not want or need His ways. We are told every single day that we can do this on our own by everything we see and hear in this world. But Jesus tells us that we are not of this world. We are of a different world. The world we are from is the world where Jesus sits at the right hand of the Father and rules. Overcomes. His world is where the hope is. This is where we find our hope.

How do we do this? We pick up our cross and follow Him. One day at a time. One moment at a time. It's hard, it's not meant to be easy. Nothing is ever easy when the outcome is great. Life is hard. Following Jesus is hard. But the end result, oh, the journey, the walking alongside Him every day. These are the rewards. How He loves to be with us, walk with us, talk with us, love us. How He loves us indeed. The hope that we find in Jesus is like no other hope that we'll find anywhere in this world. Long for it, seek it, really seek it. Do not miss the opportunity to know this Savior who loves us so very much.

Hope? Yes, there's hope in Jesus. Seek Him today. Pray to Him today. It's not easy. The road, the journey, is long, it's hard, it's lonely sometimes. But, the rewards, the hope that comes from knowing Jesus. It is absolutely priceless.

Find hope today. Long for hope today. In this life, there are indeed no guarantees, but there is Jesus. The only rock and firm foundation that we need. All else is sinking sand. Find hope today. Find Jesus today.

PRAYER: God, Jesus, today I need you. I need your hope in my life. I struggle daily with addictions, with things that push me away from you. Today, draw me near. Help me to feel your arms surrounding me, holding me, drawing me close and saying, "I'm here, I've got you, I'm holding you." Today, there is hope. Today there is Jesus. Amen.

Chapter 10
ABANDON

Chapter 10.
Abandon.

I step out of the door of the church and the sun shines on my face. I feel it's warming rays and close my eyes. I exhale. Look around and start seeing things for the first time. There are families walking in a park across the street. Playing. Enjoying the time together. A couple sits on a bench and talks. When was the last time I did that? I can't remember.

I take a walk through the park and enjoy the scene. Is this what life is supposed to be? There's this race that I've been running that doesn't work anymore. I like this. I like the idea of slowing down a little and paying attention to the details. The little things that equate to big things in the lives of other people. I think of all the time I've lost with my kids. I know they love me but I haven't been the greatest father to them. This is something that I need to change. That I will change.

I sit on a bench and watch as a dad flies a kite with his son. He holds him in his arms as the boy holds the string that holds the kite. The wind is supporting it and forcing it higher and higher into the deep blue sky above. I think back on all that Paul said about who God is. I think back on what I read last night in John. How this God above will not abandon us or leave us. He's always there. Not above but with us. Here. He's always been here, I've just been too busy with me to see Him. That changes today.

Tomorrow I'll be in Arizona. With Sarah. With the kids. I need to change all of this. Need to start over. I need to hold my son and my daughter and let them know that I won't abandon them. Need to show my wife that things are different.

I call my office. Tell my boss that it's over. I'm not coming back. They don't understand. I don't expect them to.

I can see the sun setting over the hills in the west. I get in my car and drive. Tomorrow. It all comes down to tomorrow. I find myself praying. Not even sure what to say but just praying. Talking to God in my car as this ball of light rolls down the highway. It all comes down to tomorrow.

Welcome to DAY 10.

It's Day 10. Today. We talk about our abandonment issues. Our doubt. Our struggles. Our need and want for Jesus. The chorus of this song truly wraps it up..."You're all I need, I still believe, You're never gonna leave me, You'll never abandon me."

I remember when we were recording this it started out as a Hall & Oates kind of midtempo song, then Scotty got a hold of it and this is where it landed. I love it. Again, a bit of a throwback to the eighties with just the right amount of rock and roll. The bridge is a total roller skating rink vibe. I love the lyrics in that section:

Through the wind and the fire, through the chaos and storms
To the ends of the earth, through the roses and thorns
through the deepest nights where the darkness hides
to the depths of my soul I will bravely go

Check the devotional on the next pages as we dive a little deeper into this but just know that today God's not leaving. There is no abandoning going on here. Enjoy the day!

You're all I need
I still believe
You're never gonna leave me
You'll never abandon me...

Abandon (Pettigrew/Wilbanks) © 2017 Zoovid Music, Turn It Up Productions

I'm lost and all alone, I can't find my way home
I am shaking, will i make it
I know that I may fail, the wind has left my sails
but i go on yeah, yeah i roll on
Lord reach down and rescue me

OOO OOO OOO OOO
YOU'RE ALL I NEED
OOO OOO OOO OOO
I STILL BELIEVE
OOO OOO OOO OOO
YOU'RE NEVER GONNA LEAVE ME, YOU'LL NEVER ABANDON ME

I watch the water's rise, you look me in the eye
and you hold me, yeah you hold me
it's getting hard to breathe, I'll follow where you lead
'cause your light shine's where the night blinds
 I'll make it, you wake me up

OOO OOO OOO OOO
YOU'RE ALL I NEED
OOO OOO OOO OOO
I STILL BELIEVE
OOO OOO OOO OOO
YOU'RE NEVER GONNA LEAVE ME, YOU'LL NEVER ABANDON ME

through the wind and the fire, through the chaos and storms
to the ends of the earth, through the roses and thorns
through the deepest night, where the darkness hides
to the depths of my soul i will bravely go
i'll make it, just shake me up

OOO OOO OOO OOO
YOU'RE ALL I NEED
OOO OOO OOO OOO
I STILL BELIEVE
OOO OOO OOO OOO
YOU'RE NEVER GONNA LEAVE ME, YOU'LL NEVER ABANDON ME

Abandon.

You're never gonna leave me, You'll never abandon me.

There are times when life gets tricky. We paint ourselves into corners, we drive without a map, we walk on a wire without the safety net. Funny how times like these make us draw nearer to God than the day in day out kind of stuff. God tells us that He'll never leave us or forsake us. Let's dig into a few passages of scripture that teach us more about God's presence in our lives:

Deuteronomy 31:8 – "It is the LORD who goes before you. He will be with you; he will not leave you or forsake you. Do not fear or be dismayed."

One of my favorite verses, **Joshua 1:9**, I taught this one to my kids very early on in their lives, still say it with them often: "Have I not commanded you? Be strong and courageous. Do not be frightened, and do not be dismayed, for the LORD your God is with you wherever you go."

Isaiah 41:10 – "So do not fear, for I am with you; do not be dismayed, for I am your God. I will strengthen you and help you; I will uphold you with my righteous right hand."

God with us. Emmanuel. God is here. He was here and walked the Earth. He was here and performed miracles, said things that no one else had ever said nor ever will say. He is here today with you and me. When He left after His death and resurrection, He said that He leaves with us the Holy Spirit. **John 14:26** says this, "However, the helper, the Holy Spirit, whom the Father will send in my name, will teach you everything. He will remind you of everything that I have ever told you."

So, when I sing this chorus, I sing truth. When you sing this chorus, you sing truth. We walk in perilous times. We live in a world that continually tells us that we're alone, look out for number one and push everyone else to the side to get to the top. God speaks directly against all of that and tells us to walk with Him. That He is with us and will never leave us. Concerned about your first day on a new job? God is with you. Struggling with issues with your kids? God is with you. Finals? God is with you. Getting a treatment or procedure? God is with you. The road, sometimes long, sometimes hard, all the time uncertain, is best travelled with someone. Let Jesus be that someone. God travels with us. Jesus walks alongside us.

PRAYER: God, thank you. Thank you that you never leave. That every circumstance, every heartbeat, every step, You are with me. Help me to lean more on You. Depend more on You. Fall in love with You more every day. Teach me to be patient with the process. Help me to realize that this is all part of a greater plan that You have laid out before me. Keep us in your Word and let it be a lamp unto my feet and a light unto my path. Amen.

Through the wind and the fire...

Through the chaos and storms...

Chapter 11
DON'T MISS THIS LIFE

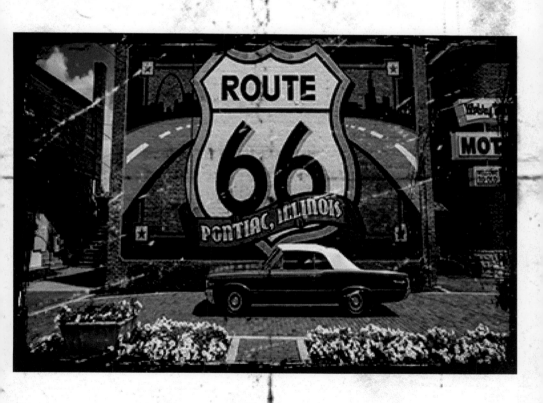

CHAPTER 11:
Don't Miss This Life

Here we go. I wake up the next morning after a long drive into the night. My mind is racing as I put the car into gear and drive. The highway takes me into a small town in Arizona called Cottonwood. I turn on route 260 and take it into town, turn right on 89A to Zalesky Road. I stop. I text Sarah. She responds within minutes. Strange....but OK. She says she's around and the kids are at school. I gulp, respond and say I'll be there in few minutes.

I bow my head as I sit on the side of the road. Say some kind of prayer and put the car in drive. I pull into the driveway on Purple Sage Trail and get out. The sun beats down from the clear blue sky. It's light warms my face. Sarah is standing there in the doorway. I wipe my hands on my pant leg and walk over to her. "Hi". I say. "Hi" she responds. Good start.

We make our way to the back patio by the pool and she asks, "OK, what's up? It's been a few months and we haven't heard from you." "I know, and for that I apologize." I dive right in. I tell her everything. I tell her about the drive, the waitress, the truck driver, Paul and his family. I tell her about Darren and his second chance and how I had a small part in that. She listens, really listens.

"Sounds like you've had quite a trip," she says. "I have. It's been quite a trip indeed." I end with telling her how I've quit my job. She smiles and looks down. "That's good. You needed to. I couldn't make you, you needed to figure that out on your own." I tell her that I'd like to start over. That there's this road that we need to get back on as a family. As husband and wife. She laughs, "Do you think it's that easy?" "No," I respond, "it's not. It will take time, and I'm here, willing to start over if you'll let me."

"The kids miss you. I miss you. We've been waiting for you, you know. I told them weeks ago that you're smarter than this and that it will just take some time." I smile and say, "you were right again, I'm sorry." I feel a tear forming in my eye. "I can't believe I've been so foolish." She takes my hand. "Tom, it's not that. We get so wrapped up in everything and aim so high for the big picture, sometimes we don't see that all we really need is right in front of us. A family, a home, kids. Everything else is a luxury."

I bow my head and sigh. She takes my other hand. I look up. There are tears in her eyes now as well. She smiles. "I've missed you. Really missed you. I see something in you that is new. Something that I haven't seen since the first day that I met you." I tell her more about Paul, about his words, about his love for God and about our prayer together. She looks out over the yard and shakes her head. "We've been going to church ever since we got out here. I needed something to ground me. Something to believe in after I couldn't believe in you. Looks like we both found it in different ways. Different paths."

"Tom," she says. "I just don't want you to miss this life. There's too much to live for. Too much here."

I get up. Walk over to the edge of the pool and turn around. I get lost in her eyes. I walk towards her, kneel down and say, "I swear, this will be a day that we'll look back on. A day that we can remember and smile. From here on out, I'm yours. I belong to you and our kids. I want nothing more than to be with you if you'll let me." She takes my face in her hands and our foreheads touch. "Yes, I believe you. I know that God is working here. I just can't believe it's really happening."

She takes my hand and leads me to the backyard. "I want to show you something," she says. We walk to the rear of the yard by the fence. There are four Arizona Cypress trees planted against it. "The kids planted these a few weeks ago." Each tree had a small sign at the base. One for each of us. "They've wanted you to be here so badly. I've been hoping and praying that these trees would represent a new life for all of us."

We walk back into the house. The sun has been moving over the deep blue sky and it's getting later in the afternoon. We step out onto the front porch. The kids school bus is coming down the street. I stand there, tears streaming down my face. Sarah looks up at me. She takes my hand and leans in to my arm. The bus stops. I see two beautiful children step off. They start walking towards the house and then recognize me on the front porch. Their eyes light up and their steps quicken. I run out onto the front walk to greet them. A father holding his arms open to hold his children. "Don't miss this life," I repeat Sarah's words in my head. As they run into my arms, I hold them tight and take a breath.

Welcome to DAY 11.

Today's a day for reflection. A day to look at what's going on and see if it's really what you want going on. I wrote this song in December of 2017. In the middle of recording the album. Scotty and I were working like crazy, 16 hour days and i remember having a conversation where we just talked about what's important and why we do what we do.

So that makes you start to think about your family, your life, decisions and a whole bunch of other stuff. So today, take a little extra time to reflect. Spend some extra time with the devotional below and the song. We only get one of these lives so let's use it as best we can for all that we can.

When I first wrote this, as you'll hear in the demo online, it was much faster. After living with it for a while, we decided to slow it down, make it a little more contemplative. I love how it came out. The acoustic guitar at the top just sets the mood. The quiet organ and the lyric. So so good.

Listen today. Listen to yourself, your heart. Don't miss it. There's too much to do and see here. The journey is hard. The journey is long. We fight it and embrace it all at the same time. Today, don't miss it. Take a breath. Don't miss this life.

Time keeps ticking
it won't slow down
Hold these moments.
And make
them count...!

Don't Miss This Life (Pettigrew) © 2017 Zoovid Music

I woke up this morning, already out of time
racing down the road that is my life
here today and gone today, tomorrow who knows
maybe I should learn to take it slow

'CAUSE THERE'S A SUN THAT IS SHINING
THERE'S A STAR TO WISH UPON
THERE'S A HAND THAT NEEDS HOLDING
THERE'S A HEART THAT CALLS YOU HOME
THERE'S A SON AND A DAUGHTER, WHO NEED YOU HERE TONIGHT
SO TAKE A BREATH, DON'T MISS THIS LIFE

so many plates are spinning, I think I'll try to set them down
and maybe find a way to be around
so I need a little mercy, a touch of your grace
give me one more chance to set this straight

'CAUSE THERE'S A SUN THAT IS SHINING
THERE'S A STAR TO WISH UPON
THERE'S A HAND THAT NEEDS HOLDING
THERE'S A HEART THAT CALLS YOU HOME
THERE'S A LOVE THAT REALLY NEEDS YOU, TO HOLD ON TIGHT TONIGHT
SO TAKE A BREATH, DON'T MISS THIS LIFE

time keeps ticking, it won't slow down
so hold these moments and make them count, I think that's what this life's about

I woke up this morning with you and the sunrise
forgiveness in your smile
the highs and lows and battered roads, the toil and the tears
through it all we're still here

'CAUSE YOU'RE THE SUN THAT IS SHINING
AND YOU'RE THE STAR I WISH UPON
AND IT'S YOUR HAND THAT I'M HOLDING
IT'S YOUR HEART THAT CALLS ME HOME
AND IT'S YOUR LOVE THAT NEVER LEAVES ME, IT'S HOLDING ME TONIGHT
I'LL TAKE A BREATH, I WON'T MISS THIS LIFE
SO JUST TAKE A BREATH, DON'T MISS THIS LIFE

Don't Miss This Life.

Take a breath, don't miss this life.

Seems fitting to end this album with this song. Time is this precious commodity. It's priceless. I remember when my kids were younger, I was incredibly focused on work. I was working a full-time job and also playing about 100 weddings per year. I was exhausted. I look back on it now and realize that I pretty much missed the first 5 years of my kid's lives because of that schedule. Those are years that I'll never get back and I regret it.

Don't Miss This Life is a song that was written while we were in the middle of working on the album. I remember having a conversation with my producer Scotty about how busy we are, about how we have so little margin in our lives. This conversation led to me heading back to New Jersey and writing this song over the Christmas break in 2017. I remember being able to just sit back, let my mind wander, pray, and focus on how good it was to have a week off to do nothing but read, watch a few movies and write. I encourage you to do this. We need time to take a breath, to just rest. Our lives are so wrapped up in work, school, family, church, the list goes on. We need time to stop. To let our wounds heal. To let our dreams come to life. To hug. To laugh. To love. These are the things we take for granted. We can do that tomorrow we say. There's always time for that next week......

Today. Do it today.

We need time in order to invest in deeper relationships. Relationships that can change things. That can change lives.

There are a few verses I wanted to add in here:

James 4:13-14 – "Now listen, you who say, Today or tomorrow we will go to such and such a town, stay there a year, conduct business, and make money. You do not know what tomorrow will bring. What is your life? You are a mist that appears for a little while and then vanishes."

Proverbs 27:1 –" Do not boast about tomorrow, for you do not know what a day may bring."

Colossians 4:5 "Behave wisely toward outsiders, making the best use of your time."

I love what Rick Warren says about time, "Time is our most precious gift because we only have a set amount of it." One of my favorite quotes on time is from J.R.R. Tolkien, "I wish it need not have happened in my time," said Frodo. "So do I," said Gandalf, "and so do all who live to see such times. But that is not for them to decide. All we have to decide is what to do with the time that is given us."

We are given each day. We are given each hour. I've decided over the past few years to make the most of the time that I have. To try to be a better father, a better husband, a better man of God. I want to be someone who leads people to the hope of Jesus. This time that He has given me, I want to use it for Him. I want to teach my kids what it means to be a follower of Jesus. I want to teach them about Jesus and about what He's done in my life. In our lives as a family.

This journey that we're on, we only have the time that's given to us. Value it. It's precious. Take hold of it and use it wisely. Pray today about the time that you have and how you will use it. Pray today that this road that God has put you on will be used in the best way that it can be used. In a way that brings Him glory.

God has a purpose for each and every one of us. He is using you today in ways that you aren't even aware of. He is perfect. His plans for you are perfect and amazing and He wants each of us to be drawn closer to Him so that we can rest in His perfect love. To experience the peace that only He can bring. Peace from anxiety, stress and worry. Peace from burn-out. Peace from every concern that comes your way every day. Don't miss it.

Don't miss this life. Don't miss the amazingness of it. God wants us to live full, rich, bold, awe-inspired lives. He wants us to interact with Him every day. To be amazed by the way He works every day. So today, open your eyes, see the goodness He brings, see the hope He brings.

This journey, this road that you're on, it's amazing. It hurts, it makes you laugh, it shines, it's lonely, it brings joy to you and others, it frustrates you, it makes you long for more. It's your journey, it's your choice. Live by faith. Live by a daily walk with Him but with all my heart, I hope that you don't miss it. I pray that you don't miss it. This life is too short to miss. Live in the joy that Jesus brings you. His love never fails and He will never, ever fail you on this journey that you're on. Let Him lead you on this road. You won't regret it.

PRAYER: God, today, help me to slow down. Help me to put down the phone or close the computer and rest in you. Give me Your peace because today I'm making time to let your peace consume me. To let your peace fill me in ways that I've never felt before. God, use me today, open my heart, eyes & arms to the needs of others. Let them see You in me and fill me with Your love. God, walk with me on this journey. I need you with me today and always. Amen.

Chapter 12
AITH AND GASOLINE
(ACOUSTIC SESSIONS)

CHAPTER 12:
Faith And Gasoline

Tom opens his eyes, sweat on his brow. He wipes his head and looks at the clock. It's 4:15am. Sarah gently sleeps beside him. He's been back for 8 months now. A lot has changed. His heart has changed, softened.

This is a regular occurrence. This waking up. Dreams have been coming and going. Trying to tell him something.

He gets up and makes a cup of coffee. The warm liquid soothes something inside him as he sits on the front porch. The cactus in the yard are tall statues reaching to the sky. The sun begins to welcome the day, pink and yellow hues start to paint the heavens , creeping like a slow fog over the mountains.

Tom waits. He lifts his head and prays. Seeking direction, seeking what's next. How many times has he done this. He feels lost yet found all at the same time. Life with his family has completed something in him but he is being pulled into more. Like a photographer patiently waiting for the right scene to open up in front of him, he sits still. Waiting. Is this what faith is? Is this how faith works?

He goes back inside and opens his computer. Fourteen emails are waiting but one stands out. It's an email from Paul with the subject line, "Thought you might be interested....". He opens it and starts reading.

Tom, hope you're well and everything worked out the way you wanted it to. I'm putting together a trip to Haiti. As part of our mission as a church, we sometimes head out and build clean water wells, houses, hospitals etc. We're leaving in a few weeks and are looking for a few more volunteers. Just throwing it out there to you. Let me know what you think.

Paul.

Hmm. Tom has just a moment to process the idea when he hears a screech outside, tires rounding a corner fast...too fast. The crash sounds like a symphony gone wrong. He rushes to the door but before he can open it, he hears a knock. He hesitates just for a moment and reaches for the door knob.....

Welcome to Day 12.

Our story with Tom continues. This story is just one in a billion stories that we come across every day. This journey, this time together is precious. Embrace it. Take time for it and enjoy it.

We start today with Faith and Gasoline, the first song on this Acoustic journey. It's a song about the journey, about the ins and outs of life and how we get so lost sometimes we can't seem to find our way out. This is where faith comes into play. I always say that this ministry runs on two things, our faith in Jesus and the gasoline that we put in the tank of our van to get to the next gig. Today, let's expand our faith, expand our beliefs and push deeper into the Word that God has given us. Faith. It's hard, complicated, frustrating, rewarding, incredible, unseen, seen and so much more.

A quick verse on faith to get us started today.

"Now faith is confidence in what we hope for and assurance about what we do not see" - Hebrews 11:1

Today. Think about your faith. Think about how faith moves in your life and if God is in that faith. I love the statement above. Faith is assurance of what we do not see. God is this physically unseen figure in our lives but it's incredible how we see Him *working* in our lives. Whenever you're feeling that You can't see God working, ask around, find folks that are walking with Him, they'll have plenty to say....

Today. Find faith.

The gaslight's shining bright
I'm drifting to the other lane
I'll roll on through the night
Into the unknown...

Chapter 13
BRING ME BACK TO LIFE AGAIN
(ACOUSTIC SESSIONS)

CHAPTER 13:
Bring Me Back To Life Again / Love Is Here.

The scene outside his home was urgent. Tom's neighbor was talking, no yelling, at him to call 911. He couldn't process it. The flames began to rise out of the car that had crashed into the Palo Verde tree in his front yard. He snapped out of it and dialed. Help was on the way.

He ran to the car and pulled open the driver's side door. It was Paul. Of all people, he had just finished reading an email from him, what was he doing here, why, how? So many unanswered questions. He pulled him out of the car just as the flames started to catch the leaves of the tree. He dragged him across the lawn and into the house.

By now, Sarah and the kids were up and watching through the front living room window. Tom told them to get back. He could hear the sirens in the distance waking the neighbors, they were going to make it before things got out of hand.

An hour later, the fire was contained and the car was being towed away. Police had asked their questions and Paul was sitting comfortably in Tom's dining room with a cup of coffee.

"Where do I begin," he started. "I found your address off of a letter that you had mailed me a few months ago with an update on your family. So glad to hear that all is working out. I'm sorry about the drama pulling into your front yard, I lost control of the car as I was coming around the last corner to your place. I had been driving all night, fell asleep at the wheel and woke up as I was coming toward your tree. So careless of me."

Tom's stare was blank as he listened. "Paul," Tom said, "Why are you here?"

Paul brought the coffee to his lips and set the cup back down on the table. The steam rose above the rim. "I'm here, Tom, because I wanted to ask you a question. I'm in the middle of gathering folks to take a trip with me and your name keeps coming up in my mind. I can't seem to shake the thought of you being there." Tom responded, "I know, I just read your email. I'm considering it." "Right," Paul said. "You know I sent that a few weeks ago." "Hmm," Tom responded, "I literally just opened it this morning, right as you were pulling up on the lawn." He smiled, "technology, sometimes it works....sometimes..."

They talked for a while longer, Paul described what he was doing and why. He was taking a trip to Haiti to help build a clean water well for a community there. He was trying to bring them back to life. Tom told Paul about how his family had kind of hit reset when he came to Arizona. They've been taking a back seat to a lot of heavy lifting and were very much back on track as a family. Paul smiled, "I knew it," he said.

They spent the day talking through the idea, what it would look like, how it would happen and who would be involved. It sounded like an opportunity very hard to pass up. Something that could actually change people's lives. Maybe change his life again.

That night Tom and Paul were looking into airfare and putting the trip together. Paul spent the night. The next morning they shook hands and Paul gave Tom a hug. So great to see all of this happening. It's incredible how God works. Paul hopped in his rental car and headed back to Indiana.

Tom shook his head as he drove away. Haiti. He'd never left the United States before. What was this going to be like?

Welcome to Day 13.

Today we're talking about the past and the future, all at the same time. Bring Me Back To Life again is a song inspired by a sermon I heard ten years ago. It was all about how Jesus, our one true source of life, is in the business of bringing us back to life again every day. His life, his strength, his peace, his wonder breathe life into us daily.

2 Corinthians 5:17 - "Therefore if anyone is in Christ, he is a new creature; the old things passed away; behold, new things have come."

New things, new life. It's all part of a relationship with Jesus. Just look at our story. Tom, the main character, is living in this new life right now. If you read through the Faith And Gasoline Journey, you know his story of redemption. Of how God put so many things in his path to lead him back to his wife and family. How the people that he came in contact with were there because God has orchestrated the whole thing.

So many people ask if that story was true. Kind of. That's the answer that I always give. It's an amalgamation of all of the stories that I hear on the road. We hear so many stories of redemption, of truth, of new life. God is in the business of helping and restoring lives. Love is here. Jesus is here.

Today, rest in the new life that Jesus has given us. The new life that his death has given us. Our hearts, our very souls are new because of his incredible love and sacrifice for us.

Bring me back to life again. Father, bring us all back to life again as we seek you more and more. Love is here. Yes, Jesus, the one true example of perfect love is here. Father, walk into our hearts and heal us. Restore us and bring us back to life.

Bring Me Back To Life Again

"I keep falling down, on this magnetic ground"

This life. All that happens. All that takes place and gets in the way. All the struggles and the pain and the joys and the greatness. It takes a toll on who we are. It gives life and takes it away.

This song continues to drive home and push through the point that in all of it, God is the one who takes our pain, out struggle, our hurt, our guilt, our stress, our shame... all of it . He takes it all and gives us the strength to go on. To continue the fight. To continue the journey.

Today. You may be struggling. You may be hurting. You may be stressed or have anxiety pushing you to a place that you don't want to go. Dig deep into these verses:

"The Spirit of God has made me and the breath of the Almighty gives me life." - Job 33:4

"You will make known to me the path of life, in Your presence is fullness of joy, in Your right hand there are pleasures forever." - Psalm 16:11

God is our refuge and strength, an ever-present help in trouble. Therefore we will not fear, though the earth give way and the mountains fall into the heart of the sea, though its waters roar and foam and the mountains quake with their surging." - Psalm 46: 1-3

Dig around in the Bible. Find more promises that bring us back to life, find more promises that confirm to us that God is with us, God is here, God is fighting for you,for me.

So today, ask God to take it. Ask Him to bring you back to life.

Take everything that I have seen, take everything that isn't me, take everywhere that I have been and bring me back to life again
Take everything that I have know, the good and the bad, the hurt that shows
I know I can't do this on my own, so bring me back to life again....

He is with us. He is waiting for you.

God, today, we lift Your name. We lift our hands and our hearts to the promises that You have given us.You declare over and over and over again in your word that You love us, care for us and are walking with us through it all. We claim those promises today. Bring us life Lord, Bring us hope. Bring us love. Bring us all that You have in store for us as we pray for life today.

Bring us back to life today.

Bring Me Back To Life Again (Pettigrew) © 2019 Zoovid Music

Once upon a time is not quite what i find
when i look ahead at how this will end
i'm so wrapped up in me, i can't see that i need
to hit reset and start this over again
i just want to know, can you...

TAKE EVERYTHING THAT I HAVE SEEN, TAKE EVERYTHING THAT ISN'T ME
TAKE EVERYWHERE THAT I HAVE BEEN AND BRING ME BACK TO LIFE AGAIN

a new beginning is what you are bringing
another chance to help me believe
'cause i keep falling down on this magnetic ground
still i get up, at least up to my knees
i just want to know, can you...

TAKE EVERYTHING THAT I HAVE SEEN, TAKE EVERYTHING THAT ISN'T ME
TAKE EVERYWHERE THAT I HAVE BEEN AND BRING ME BACK TO LIFE AGAIN
TAKE EVERYTHING THAT I HAVE KNOWN, THE GOOD AND THE BAD
THE HURT THAT SHOWS
I KNOW I CAN'T DO THIS ON MY OWN, SO BRING ME BACK TO LIFE AGAIN

i won't pretend that i can make it on my own
so won't you send me down a little bit of heaven in my life

TAKE EVERYTHING THAT I HAVE SEEN, TAKE EVERYTHING THAT ISN'T ME
TAKE EVERYWHERE THAT I HAVE BEEN AND BRING ME BACK TO LIFE AGAIN
TAKE EVERYTHING THAT I HAVE KNOWN, THE GOOD AND THE BAD
THE HURT THAT SHOWS
I KNOW I CAN'T DO THIS ON MY OWN, SO BRING ME BACK TO LIFE AGAIN

Chapter 14
LOVE IS HERE
(ACOUSTIC SESSIONS)

Chapter 14.
Love Is Here.

Welcome to Day 14.

"Love walks into my house and turns the lights back on."

The opening line from the song "Love Is Here". There's so much to talk about in this song, I wanted to take another look at it and put together another devotional for it.

This line about love walking into my house and turning the lights back on. I do love it and especially love the sentiment of it. We are all so wrapped up in so many different things that pull us down into the mire of the world. To think about the love of Jesus walking in the front door of our lives and our hearts and just clicking the switch is.... refreshing to say the least.

"And so we know and rely on the love God has for us. God is love. Whoever lives in love, lives in God, and God in them. - 1 John 4:16

How very important love is in our lives. How important it is to embrace it and welcome it into our hearts. Jesus' loves knows no bounds, knows no limits. How important it is to live in love and live in God.

"We love because He first loved us" 1 John 4:19

Again, such an important example that God set for us, that Jesus set for us. That we would be able to actually love because of the example and vision that He set forth for us. Love leads us closer and closer to Him and closer and closer to each other. Let love reign and rule in your life today.

"Love walks into my doubts when trust is all but gone"

Trust. Something that is so easily broken and so incredibly hard to win back. Our doubts our fears, our losses are all trumped by the love that God continues to pour into us each and every day. Each and every moment of our lives.

Embrace it. Today, embrace love, embrace joy. Embrace all that He has in store for you.

Love is here. Love is now. Love is all that will remain. Love is all I want to know. It's the promise that I hold and you don't have to fear.

Love is here.

Chapter 15
UNDERTOW
(ACOUSTIC SESSIONS)

CHAPTER 15:
Undertow.

The drill hit the dry earth with a powdery thump. It started to turn and Tom watched eagerly.

This was their fourth day in Haiti. It was 92 degrees and hot. The second day they had begun drilling, it didn't work. The drill bit had cracked about 30 feet down and they had to stop. The drill team was headed up by a burly young man named Evens. He had been doing this for about 7 years, had a lot of success and was a pro. He was part of an organization called Water For Life and believed in the life changing power of water. Tom liked him immediately.

Evens was pushing hard to make this drill pierce through the earth. The deepest well that he had ever drilled was 810 feet. They were hoping that they didn't have to go that deep on this day. The sunrise that morning in Duranton, a rural town in the Grand'Anse department of Haiti, was beautiful. Tom was seeing things he had never seen before. Meeting people that he didn't even know existed. These were days that he never thought he'd see.

Paul came over and put his hand on Tom's shoulder. "Incredible isn't it?" he said. "Yeah", Tom replied, "Thanks so much for bringing me. I'll never be the same. I would have loved to have brought...."

Before he could finish there was a loud cry from Evens and then....it was raining. Water was spewing everywhere and Evens jumped down off the drill rig and ran over to Tom. "We got it!" he exclaimed. The whole crew had their heads pointed towards the sky and were basking in the sun shower that Evens had just supplied. A rainbow pierced through the rain. Life. They were dancing, singing, and praising. Hands lifted high and hope in their eyes. It was an absolutely euphoric scene. Tom had tears in his eyes, this changed everything.

That night Paul, Tom and Evens were sitting by the fire outside of their tents. "Tomorrow we leave," Paul said. "This has been one for the books. So great to have you with us Tom." Tom just smiled, knowing that if he said anything his voice would be unsure of itself. Paul continued, "You see Evens, Tom has a story that so many of us Americans have. Working like crazy, not sure what we're working for, not spending enough time with family, friends. It's a trap that many of us get so wrapped up in. It's the undertow that pulls us further and further away from God. It's the impossible cycle that so many people get sucked into." Evens looked over and said these words in his thick Haitian accent, "All of those things are certainly appealing, but for me, for my crew here, we bring life. We want to see life given to those who don't have it. Today we did that."

On the plane ride home the next day Tom's mind was racing. He took a deep breath and started praying. Praying that God would lead him where he was supposed to go. Where he was supposed to be. He opened his eyes and saw Paul's white knuckles on the armrest next to his. He looked up and saw the flight attendant running to the front of the plane....

Welcome to Day 15.

Ah, the undertow. We all get stuck in it. So many of us fight and fight and so often lose. It takes faith to fight the undertow. Faith in what God has planned for us. Faith in our own surrender. Faith in our ability to stop and let go of the wheel.

I find myself daily struggling with the undertow. We get so wrapped up in work, life, kids, school, church, TV, social media, that we don't find time to spend with God. It's an alluring and tempting world we live in. So many distractions, so many things that take our mind and our hearts off of the one thing that our minds and hearts should be absorbed with.

A few verses to remind us of the fact that God will never let us go. Ever.

I have set the LORD continually before me; Because He is at my right hand, I will not be shaken. - Psalm 16:8

Jesus Christ is the same yesterday and today and forever. - Hebrews 13:8

What then shall we say to these things? If God is for us, who is against us? - Romans 8:31

He is before all things, and in Him all things hold together. - Colossians 1:17

For every house is built by someone, but the builder of all things is God. - Hebrews 3:4

There are so many more references and verses that back up this point. God will never leave us. He is always here. Google it. Search for it. Don't take my word for it. Find your own evidence.

The undertow is strong. It never lets up and never stops coming. We have to make our foundation stronger. We have to have our minds and our hearts set on one thing. Jesus.

Focus today. Resist the undertow today and fight.

Chapter 16
EFLECTION OF YOU / ME
(ACOUSTIC SESSIONS)

CHAPTER 16:
Relection of You / Me.

There are moments in your life where things just get out of control. This was one of them.

Tom looked forward and felt the nose of the plane take a steep dive. He looked at Paul. His eyes were closed, deep in prayer. The service cart rolled past their aisle and made a beeline for the first class section. A baby was crying in the back somewhere. If there were dogs on this plane...they would be barking.

Tom closed his eyes, thought of Sarah, his children. All that's happened over the past few days. About how life was just getting good. How life was just getting to a place where he thought he was in control a little bit. His mind takes him back to the day when he first started this second chapter of his life. To the waitress who said that there's a love that holds it all together. He was still trying to understand that completely but he felt he was getting closer. This past week in Haiti showed him a new kind of love that he didn't know existed. Let alone existed in his heart. His mind showed him his deep love for his kids, his deep love for his wife and his deep love for the new life that he's found.

Two nights ago in Haiti, Evens, was talking to Tom about love. About how the love that we have for our kids, our families, is dwarfed in comparison to the love that God has for us. It's a love that we can't even begin to comprehend. Tom needed that, he heard it and needed it deep in his soul. His life was still changing.

He was startled out of this daydream to the sound of the captain coming on saying that they are going to have to make an emergency landing in Tamaulipas, Mexico. There's an abandoned airport there that will have to suffice.

Tom and Paul both put their heads between their knees and prayed. The wheels hit the dirt runway hard and the plane shook. The pit of Tom's stomach lurched the way it would on a steep drop in a roller coaster. The plane slows down and suddenly there's silence. Everyone is stunned. Then cheering and laughter. Tom smiles to Paul and they make their way slowly off the plane.

After a night in a local hotel, they find a rental car and decide to drive the rest of the way home. The journey continues says Tom to Paul. Yes it does, he replies.

The drive is long, but gives Tom the time he needs to think and think more. He gets into quite a few deep conversations with Paul about how this week has changed him and how he is feeling like the last 8 months has been so different from the time before. Paul speaks on the redeeming love of Jesus and Tom feels like he's found that love in a way that he never knew existed. Paul talks about how we need to be a reflection of Jesus here and how he and Tom for the past few days were exactly that. Changing things that need to be changed. Taking the focus off of ourselves and putting it on others. Being the me that God made us to be.

The white lines flash by and Tom's life will never be the same again.

Welcome to Day 16.

Today is a day to think. When you've had a near death experience it leads you to think more about life. About how you live your life and how you spend your time. Our main character here is in the midst of that thought right now for sure.

How about you? How are you spending your time? Your work time? Your time with your family? Are you present when they are with you or are you distracted? For years, I was distracted. It was hard for me to not look at my phone, my computer. To not have thoughts racing through my head about work, about ministry, about everything except what I was supposed to be focusing on. My God, my family, myself.

Today. Think about how you spend your time. How you can be the you that God has made you to be. We've all been designed in an incredibly beautiful way. In a way that only God could orchestrate. Be the YOU that God wants you to be.

Pray today that God would reveal Himself to you. That God would reveal the plans that He has for you. That God would reveal to you that you are an incredibly beautiful person and that there is only one you who can do what you do.

God, in the midst of it all, be with us. Let us be a reflection of who You are in our lives.

Chapter 17
I AM READY NOW
(ACOUSTIC SESSIONS)

CHAPTER 17:
I Am Ready Now.

There's something about the morning on a desolate highway in Arizona. The way the colors bounce off the mountains and paint these beautiful strokes of pink and orange. The way the skyline makes this black uneven border around it all. There are no easy edges to paint inside of, no straight lines to coast along. Kind of like life. It's a kind of beauty that can't be truly described without seeing it or experiencing it.

Tom looks over in the passengers seat. Paul is sleeping. They've been driving for 2 hours, leaving early to try and make it home in time for lunch.

The road passes silently beneath the car.

Tom is still trying to piece together the past few days. It's been a whirlwind like nothing he had ever experienced before. Life has changed in these days. He was speaking to Sarah last night. She listened. Tom could hear her softly crying as he talked through all of the details. "God sometimes takes us down paths we don't think we would ever travel," she was saying. "These are the things that define us and shape our lives. Shape our character and our future."

They pulled into the driveway at around 1pm. Tom's kids ran out to greet him and they hugged for a long time. Sarah smiled as she saw them. She came over to join the family. Paul smiled. He knew things were changing in an amazing way.

In the days and weeks that followed, Tom and Sarah's life changed. Tom started working for a non-profit that built clean water wells in Haiti and beyond. He was amazed at the change he could make in the lives of so many others with so little. Paul continued to check in. He and Tom stayed very good friends in the years ahead.

He remembers one night a few days after he and Paul arrived home from Haiti. He was sitting on the back porch swing with Sarah. They were talking softly about change. About how things could and would change. He sat quietly and then said, "I am ready now. I'm ready to take the leap, take that step and move forward with it. God is in control here, God is in control here."

They held hands as the crickets sang a chorus to the heavens and the stars blinked softly in the night sky.

Welcome to Day 17.

Are you ready?

It's a question that all of us face or will face at one time or many times in our lives.

This whole journey has been about faith. About how we need to lean deeper and deeper into God. Into the plans that He has for us and into our relationship with Him.

Being ready. Being willing to change a few things in our lives in order to change a few things in others peoples lives is a sacrifice. Jesus knows about sacrifice. We live because He lives.

A few words on faith and planning.

Jeremiah 29:11 - "For I know the plans I have for you," declares the LORD, "plans to prosper you and not to harm you, plans to give you hope and a future."

Hebrews 13:20-21 - "Now may the God of peace, who through the blood of the eternal covenant brought back from the dead our Lord Jesus, that great Shepherd of the sheep, equip you with everything good for doing his will, and may he work in us what is pleasing to him, through Jesus Christ, to whom be glory for ever and ever."

It tells us right in the scriptures that God has plans for us. That God will equip us. That God will be there with us. Inspire us. Guide us. Make us ready. Use us.

I don't know about you but I want to be used by God. Used to make a change in this world and make a change in the small community of influence that I have.

Are you ready? Are you ready for what's next? God has so much in store for you. For me. We just need to lean deeper and deeper into Him and His word so that we can be ready to act when He puts His plan into motion. Scary? Yes. Uncertain? Yes. Fulfilling? Absolutely.

So. Thank you for being here. Thanks for being a part of this journey. I hope it changed things a little for you. I hope it made you think more and decide to do some things differently.

Enjoy the albums. Thanks for your support and for being a part of this ministry. We couldn't do it without you.

I AM READY NOW (Pettigrew)

VERSE 1:
Like the waves against the bow, I'm pushing through this now
I know your hand guides my way
It don't matter where I've been or how my hearts unhinged
I know you see beyond the scrapes, and for the first time I feel awake

CHORUS:
I am ready now, to see what life's about, I've waited all these years to stand right here
I am ready now, I've made it through the how, goodbye to all I've known
Hello to hope. There's no doubt, that I am ready now

VERSE 2:
She was waiting in that line, she'd been there a thousand times
The doctor called her in, she prayed
He said here we are again, but this time she caught his grin
She hit her knees when she heard him say, "today your life is about to change"
and she said....

CHORUS:
Remember when I said I wouldn't make it I couldn't take it
I'd given up on every dream I had
Remember when you said you'd fight for me, you'd cry for me, you'd die for me
You'd give me my life back, you gave me my life back

Like the rain that ends the draught or the sun that melts the clouds
I know that hope is here today

CHORUS:
I am ready now, to see what life's about, I've waited all these years to stand right here
I am ready now, I've made it through the how, goodbye to all I've known
Hello to hope. There's no doubt, that I am ready now
There's no doubt that I am ready

Chapter 18
FINAL THOUGHTS...

CAN I SAVE A LIFE? The short answer.....yes....

We heard a lot about the power of clean water in the Faith And Gasoline Acoustic Journey section. The clean water wells that are built truly do save lives and change communities. A few facts about clean water:

- 1 in 9 people in the world don't have access to clean water

- in developing countries, up to 80% of illnesses are linked to poor water and sanitation conditions

- 783 million people worldwide do not have access to clean water

- every minute a newborn dies from an infection due to lack of clean water

- you can change this, not for everyone but for one child. It's easy.

I have partnered with Holt International and am anxious to speak with you about how you can sponsor a child for just $34 per month. That $34 gives children and their families access to clean drinking water, food, health care clothing and so much more. For some it's the difference between life and death. Today, you can make a difference, you can make a change in the life of someone you may never meet this side of heaven. You can make a difference. **Send me a note at dave@davepettigrew.net** if you'd like to talk through the process. It's easy and simple. Just five minutes is all we need to get you set up.....

If you'd like to see who needs your help. Go to this website:

http://www.sponsorachildnow.net

Your help, your generosity today can save a life. Imagine meeting a child whose life you've saved. Imagine meeting their family. Imagine being the difference in someones life today.

Let's talk. Let's join together and save lives together. I can't wait to hear from you.

Thanks for reading the Faith And Gasoline Journey devotional book. My hope is that over the course of this book you've come in contact with feelings, hopes, dreams and desires in your own life. The point of all of this is to draw us all closer and closer to Jesus. I hope this helped in some small way.

Lean into Him today. Draw near to Him and He will draw near to you.

The following few pages are pages to take notes, jot down ideas, talk to yourself about what you've learned and what you want to do. Maybe it's a place for you to start your own journey. Maybe it's a place to write down a few things that need to change in your own life. Maybe.....

I hope you find what you're looking for. It all starts and ends with Jesus.

i'll go where you lead
maybe all that i need
is a little faith and gasoline...

Stay connected!

Be sure to grab the music, merch and more at
http://www.buydpstuff.com

Join our community at http://www.mondaynightworship.com

Support our ministry monthly and become a monthly partner.
Dive deeper into the Bible with our online community and get
daily devotions, exclusive access to videos, advance music, video
devotions and more at http://www.joindavesband.com

If you're struggling with addiction, go to
http://www.thereishopemovement.com to start your journey to
recovery

Have a question or comment, email me at dave@davepettigrew.net

Find me on social media:
http://www.facebook.com/davepettigrewmusic
http://www.instagram.com/davepettigrew
http://www.youtube.com/dpettigrew
http://www.twitter.com/davepettigrew

**CONTINUE THE JOURNEY ONLINE. SIGN UP FOR FREE
DEVOTIONALS ONLINE AND GET ACCESS TO ALL THE
BONUS CONTENT HERE:**

http://www.faithandgasolinejourney.com
http://www.theacousticalbumjourney.com

http://www.davepettigrew.net

FAITH AND GASOLINE JOURNAL

FAITH AND GASOLINE JOURNAL

FAITH AND GASOLINE JOURNAL

FAITH AND GASOLINE JOURNAL

FAITH AND GASOLINE JOURNAL

FAITH AND GASOLINE JOURNAL

FAITH AND GASOLINE JOURNAL

FAITH AND GASOLINE JOURNAL

FAITH AND GASOLINE JOURNAL

FAITH AND GASOLINE JOURNAL

FAITH AND GASOLINE JOURNAL

FAITH AND GASOLINE JOURNAL

FAITH AND GASOLINE JOURNAL

FAITH AND GASOLINE JOURNAL

_____

_____

_____

_____

_____

_____

_____

_____

_____

_____

_____

_____

FAITH AND GASOLINE JOURNAL